D1590595

Double-Consciousness/Double Bind

Double-Consciousness/Double Bind

Theoretical Issues in Twentieth-Century Black Literature

SANDRA ADELL

University of Illinois Press   Urbana and Chicago

Library of Congress Cataloging-in-Publication Data
Adell, Sandra.
    Double-consciousness/double bind : theoretical issues in twentieth-
century black literature / Sandra Adell.
        p. cm.
    Includes bibliographical references and index.
    ISBN 0-252-02109-6 (alk. paper : cloth)
        1. American literature—Afro-American authors—History and
criticism—Theory, etc.   2. American literature—20th century—
History and criticism—Theory, etc.   3. Literature and society—
United States—History—20th century.   4. Afro-Americans—
Intellectual life.   5. Afro-Americans in literature.   I. Title.
PS153.N5A29   1994
810.9'896073'0904—DC20   93-49578
                                                              CIP

for próspero saíz

Contents

Acknowledgments

I would like to thank the University of Wisconsin–Madison's Graduate Research Committee for granting me the summer support I needed to complete this project. I am grateful to Lisa Warne-Magro for seeing to it that things went according to schedule. A very special thank you to my manuscript editor, Rita D. Disroe, for her expert copyediting and for her insightful comments about the craft of writing.

Introduction

      In recent years the complex ensemble of literature, literary criticism, theory, and philosophy has been problematized. What has emerged from this problematic is what is most often ignored or forgotten by an increasing number of critics and theorists of literature written by and about blacks; namely, that black literary criticism and theory, like literary criticism and theory in general, relies heavily on the Western philosophical tradition. This reliance on the Western philosophical tradition has important implications for black-specific theories of writing, for, as I will show, this dependency calls into question the very possibility of such specificity. Unfortunately, however, as the current sharp debates among some of the leading critics and theorists of black literature have demonstrated, the problems of the philosophical grounds of black literature are often subordinated, if they are raised at all, to problems of defining the proper social and political postures of those black writers engaged in the critical and theoretical enterprise.

The debate that was initiated by the 1987 publication in *New Literary History* of Joyce A. Joyce's "The Black Canon: Reconstructing Black American Literary Criticism"[1] is an example of how the theoretical positions certain black critics have chosen for their work on African-American literature have created a crisis in the discipline itself. In "The Black Canon," Joyce argues that an anthology of literature and criticism co-edited by Michael Harper and Robert Stepto[2] marks a departure from the traditional role of African-American literary critics as the "point of consciousness for his or her people" and that "black post-structuralist" critics like Houston A. Baker, Jr., and Henry Louis Gates, Jr., have adopted "a linguistic system and an accompanying world view" from structuralism, post-structuralism, and postmodernism that estrange black writers from their audiences. Joyce feels that these critics' distant, sterile and pseudoscientific language "challenges" their intellect and "dulls" them to "the realities of the sensual, communicative function of language." What

Joyce prescribes—much (black) theorizing about (black/white) criticism is openly prescriptive—is that as the circulator and preserver of racial/ communal values, the black literary critic, once accepted by "mainstream society, should question the values that will be transmitted through his or her work."[3]

In "Who's Zoomin' Who: The New Black Formalism," another critic, Norman Harris, echoes Joyce's concern.[4] He criticizes Robert Stepto and Henry Louis Gates for working out of a Eurocentric theoretical framework that threatens the integrity of the Afro-American literary tradition by ignoring its social and political foundations. Harris works from the assumption that there is an "epistemological legitimacy" to literature that is congruent with the way people of African descent have traditionally conceived and validated their perceptions of the world. Emphasizing the "vagaries and beauties of Afro-American life," he argues that in deemphasizing the social or political, Stepto and Gates are engaging in a "New Formalism" that "disfigures the literature it discusses while trivializing the dreams of Afro-Americans in the world."[5] According to Harris, this "New Black Formalism" distorts the *proper* reading, understanding, and interpretation of African-American literature. As an alternative, he suggests an *Afrocentric* critical framework such as the one elaborated by Stephen Henderson in the introduction to *Understanding the New Black Poetry*. For Harris, Henderson's notion of saturation, that is, "the communication of Blackness and the fidelity to the observed or intuited truth of the Black Experience in the United States," opens up the possibility for readings of (black) texts that "simultaneously embrace and transcend intertextuality."[6] Afrocentrism would therefore become the critical *Other* of European literary discourse.

These concerns about the social and political in critical readings of African-American literature are not new. In 1971, Addison Gayle addressed these same issues in *The Black Aesthetic,* an anthology that includes almost a century of critical essays by black writers and academicians. Yet as I will show, while the social and political contexts of black literature undeniably reflect aspects of the realities of the lives of black people, to privilege them in critical and theoretical discourses as Joyce, Harris, and other African-American critics who share their concerns have done, is to risk falling back upon some of the naïve formulas and imperatives of the Black Aesthetic.

Thus said, I do not mean to suggest that the Black Aesthetic was a worthless critical endeavor. On the contrary, the Black Aesthetic, which grew out of the Black Arts movement of the 1960s, helped to define the contours of the African-American literary tradition as we understand it today. It also helped to elaborate and refine the theories of black literary criticism received from an earlier generation of black writers. I maintain rather that because of its ideological biases, the Black Aesthetic failed to address a number of fundamental issues arising from the intersection it had constructed by virtue of its name—the Black *Aesthetic,* between black literature and Western philosophy.

Furthermore, in the wake of structuralism, post-structuralism, and deconstruction, the black critic in the 1990s is confronted with questions and imperatives that are different from the ones that preoccupied the black aestheticians. For example, Addison Gayle writes in his introduction to *The Black Aesthetic* that the task of the black critic is to question the extent to which a play, a poem, or a novel has helped to transform an "American Negro into an African-American or a black man."[7] What is left unchallenged by Gayle, and by Joyce and Harris as well, is whether, in this age of ready-made "high tech" images, literature and its critical and theoretical discourses have the power to effect such a social, political, and psychological transformation.

These kinds of critical imperatives also risk implying, as Harris does, that African-Americans share a holistic perception of the world, that more than twenty-five million people perceive the world's complexity in a monolithic way. These imperatives in effect close off differences and ignore the very complex problems of language, reading, understanding, and interpretation that have become, at least over the past two decades, as much the subject of literary theory as the literary text itself. Harris has certainly not considered how such complexities affect his own argument: in order to "transcend" intertextuality, as he suggests, one must somehow transcend language itself, since language is always intertextual. Moreover, to privilege the social and political as Joyce and Harris have done is to obscure the manner in which all critical discourses, including their own, are grounded in philosophical premises that may subvert their intentions.

Through a series of close readings of works by a number of major twentieth-century black writers and critics, I seek to intervene in the debate that was initiated by Joyce's "The Black Canon" in order to reflect upon the extent to which twentieth-century black literature and criticism are implicated in the ensemble of Western literature and philosophy. Until the relation between the black literary tradition and this ensemble is better understood, the field of black literary studies will not advance beyond these disputes over the presumed opposition between the social and political and the aesthetic or beyond the great Afrocentric/Eurocentric divide.

Although the guiding concept for my reflections is W. E. B. Du Bois's notion of "double-consciousness," my critical methodology is comparative. I engage the insights of a number of African, African-American, and European theorists, including those of Jacques Derrida, whose deconstruction radically intervenes into Western critical, theoretical, and philosophical discourses in order to further the questioning of, among other things, structures fundamental to political and social oppression.

Derrida has demonstrated through his principle of supplementarity that writing, which is the essence of all literary traditions and canons, always adds to or substitutes for previous writing. This judgment implies that a text, any text, despite its social, political, or ideological context, and despite its claims to truth, is always a multiplicity of other texts. It is part of a determined textual system, with its own language and logic, into which those writing inscribe themselves, and by which they allow themselves to be governed. Critical reading is an important aspect of this system since its aim, at least according to Derrida, should be to produce a signifying structure based on the relationship between what the writer "does and does not command of the language that he uses."[8]

Likewise, the language and logic of this textual system structure, shape, and govern the social and political institutions identified by Joyce and Harris. For this reason, Joyce and Harris are no less implicated in this system than Stepto, Baker, and Gates. Their writing, like all critical writing, exceeds the limits of their ideology. In developing an ideological rhetoric for criticizing the theorists, Joyce and Harris must *supplement* their critical discourses by appropriating terms and concepts from the methodologies they call into question. Joyce's use of the word *canon* in the title of her essay and Harris's faith in the "deep structural continuities" of the African-American experience as defined by anthropology, linguistics, psychology, and history, secure them firmly within the Western metaphysical tradition.[9] The patterns of language they use are no less governed by the textual system within which they are inscribed than those of other present and past African-American practitioners of literary criticism and theory. One need only read what is arguably the first critical essay on literature published by a black American, Anna Cooper's 1892 "One Phase of American Literature" or W. E. B. Du Bois's *The Souls of*

Black Folk to see that in African-American critical discourses, that textual system is from the beginning strongly Eurocentric.

In her critique of American literature, Anna Cooper uses the languages of romanticism and of *mimesis* to develop a theory of representation and to comment on the relationship between writers and critics and writing. She reiterates a question that was once asked by Sydney Smith, "Who ever reads an American book?"[10] to make her point that not until American writers broke their dependency on the literature, the landscape, and "the insular and monarchic customs and habits of thought of old England" did American literature cease to be a mere imitation of English literature and achieve the "something characteristic and *sui generis*" that makes a "product" worthy of the term literature. Their writing became "national" and "representative" as they entered more fully and "sympathetically" into the "distinctive life of their nation, and endeavored to reflect and picture its homeliest pulsations and its elemental components" (176). The problem is that with the exception of Harriet Beecher Stowe whose *Uncle Tom's Cabin* "England couldn't parallel," they didn't enter deeply enough, according to Cooper. Their writing failed to reflect and picture the "one objective reality" that distinguished the American landscape from that of England—the presence of African-American slaves:

> no artist for many a generation thought them worthy the sympathetic study of a model. No Shakespeare arose to distil from their unmatched personality and unparalleled situations the exalted poesy and crude grandeur of an immortal Caliban. Distinct in color, original in temperament, simple and unconventionalized in thought and action their spiritual development and impressionability under their novel environment would have furnished, it might seem, as interesting a study in psychology for the poetic pen, as would the gorges of the Yosemite to the inspired pencil. (178)

Cooper's poetics, like that of Wordsworth and the English romantics, is strongly influenced by the idea that the writer should follow the example of the painter and always "keep the eye on the subject."[11]

The writers who make up the first of the two artistic categories Cooper constructs are those "in whom the artistic or poetic instinct is uppermost—those who write to please—or rather who write because *they* please; who simply paint what they see, as naturally, as instinctively, and as irresistibly as the bird sings—with no thought of an audience—singing because it loves to sing,—singing because God, nature, truth sings through it. For such writers, to be true to themselves and true to Nature is the only canon" (181). In this context, Cooper defines *truth* in terms of feelings, the imagination, and sense perception. Truth is "merely the representation of the sensations and experiences of our personal environment, colored and vivified—fused into consistency and crytallized [*sic*] into individuality in the crucible of our own feelings and imaginations" (177). Her definition of truth corresponds to what Kant in the *Critique of Judgment* calls "beautiful art." It implies a "freedom in the play of our cognitive faculties," which for Kant is a necessary condition for the production of beautiful art.

Kant writes that for art to be beautiful it must show no trace of the "rule" that guides the artist's mental powers. He calls that rule genius and defines it as a talent for producing exemplary models that "serve as a standard or rule of judgment for others," but for which no definite rule can be given regarding its own production. "It cannot describe or indicate scientifically how it brings about its products, but it gives the rule just as nature does. Hence the author of a product for which he is indebted to his genius does not know himself how he has come by his ideas."[12] For Cooper, *Uncle Tom's Cabin* is the exemplary model against which she measures the success of subsequent nineteenth-century American writers who chose "the Negro" as their subject.

Cooper places most of the American writers who followed Stowe— along with "Milton in much of his writing, Carlyle in all of his, often our own Whittier, the great reformer-poet, and Lowell together with such novelists as E. P. Roe, Bellamy, Tourgee and some others" into her second artistic category (183). Cooper argues that, unlike her "artists for art's sweet sake," her group-two writers were all guided by the prevailing — *isms* of the day rather than by whatever talent (or genius) they might have possessed. That is why their writing failed to "withstand the ravages of time. 'Isms' have their day and pass away. New necessities arise with new conditions and the emphasis has to be shifted to suit the times" (183). But Cooper insists that the shift must not be to the detriment of art. Her criticism of many of the writers who, for whatever reason, chose "the Negro" as their subject has to do with the extent to which they either "perverted" their art to serve their ends, or lacked sufficient knowledge about their subject to produce works equal to that of *Uncle Tom's Cabin*. In her opinion, they lacked Mrs. Stowe's "power" because they had not studied their subject with her "humility and love." Some, according to Cooper, had not studied their subject at all. They simply casually observed their cooks and coachmen and then proceeded to write what they thought they knew about "the Negro" and the problem of the color line. Others, like Albion Tourgee, lacked what she feels is essential for producing good fiction: the ability to "'think oneself imaginatively into the experiences of others'" (185). As a result, Tourgee's characters are all "little Tourgees — they preach his sermons and pray his prayers," but they bear little resemblance to the real-life figures they are supposed to represent (189).

Cooper refers to the protagonist in *Pactolus Prime* as an example of how Tourgee's characters represent none other than Tourgee himself: "His caustic wit, his sledge hammer logic, his incisive criticism, his righteous indignation, all reflect the irresistible arguments of the great pleader for the Negro; and all the incidents are arranged to enable this bootblack to impress on senators and judges, lawyers and divines, his plea for justice to the Negro, along with the blacking and shine which he skillfully puts on their aristocratic toes" (189).

Tourgee's fiction, like that of G. W. Cable, belongs to what Cooper calls the "didactic or polemic class" of writing.[13] It reveals nothing of the being of its presumed subject. It simply reasserts the politics of its author, albeit a politics guided by a noble and just cause. Cooper gratefully acknowledges the efforts of writers like Tourgee who felt compelled to "champion the black man's cause." But she insists that the writer's intention should in no way impede the critical process: "This criticism is not altered by our grateful remembrance of those who have heroically taken their pens to champion the black man's cause. But even here we may remark that a painter may be irreproachable in motive and as benevolent as an angel in intention, nevertheless we have a right to compare his copy with the original and point out in what respects it falls short or is overdrawn; and he should thank us for doing so" (187).

Cooper is not nearly as charitable in her criticism of William Dean Howells, who by the 1880s was generally considered a major American novelist and literary critic. She sums up Howells's "copy" of the Negro in a single phrase: "Mr. Howells does not know what he is talking about" (201). She goes on to declare it "an insult to humanity and a sin against God" for anyone to publish the kinds of "sweeping generalizations" Howells makes in *An Imperative Duty*,[14] a short novel about the woes of miscegenation that first appeared in 1891 as a serial in *Harper's Monthly*.

Cooper complains that Howells makes the mistake of representing the colored church folk whom his octoroon heroine encounters and finds so repulsive as "'evidently . . . representing *the best colored society*'" (202). Unwittingly, perhaps, Cooper exposes the class biases that existed among the black intellectual elite of her time when she criticizes Howells for his lack of knowledge about the more cultivated class of colored people and for basing his portrayals on his observations of colored "menials and lazzaroni. . . . He has not seen, and therefore cannot be convinced that there exists a quiet, self-respecting, dignified class of easy life and manners . . . of cultivated tastes and habits, and with no more in common with the class of his acquaintance than the accident of complexion, — beyond a sympathy with their wrongs, or a resentment at being socially and morally classified with them" (207).

In Cooper's judgment, Howells fails to present a fuller picture of black people because he has "studied his subject merely from the outside." He therefore lacks the requisite requirement for good fiction: he cannot "'think himself imaginatively' into the colored man's place" (209). Cooper concludes her essay by asserting that only the black man can do that. Her hope in 1892 was that by the time she died[15] she would see "a black man honestly and appreciatively portraying both the Negro as he is, and the white man, occasionally, as seen from the Negro's standpoint" (225). By the time her essay was published, Charles Chesnutt had already met that task in the novel; Frances Harper had gained considerable attention as a poet; and W. E. B. Du Bois was well on his way to becoming one of the twentieth century's most influential American scholars.[16]

Chapter 1 of this book investigates the metaphysical foundations of Du Bois's famous formulation of "double-consciousness." This research will be the first time anyone has shown in detail how this seminal black writer's notion of "double-consciousness" emerges from the philosophy of Hegel as it is articulated in the *Phenomenology of Spirit*. This analysis is important because Du Bois's notion of "double-consciousness" is what many of the black writers of the Harlem Renaissance, Négritude, the Black Arts movement on through to the present have attempted, at least implicitly, to reconcile through their literary texts and criticism.

In Chapter 2, I analyze how Léopold Senghor and Aimé Césaire use Du Bois as a point of departure for their theories of Négritude, and how they rely on the Eurocentric/anthropological/metaphysical tradition in

their efforts to establish an ontology of blackness. I also address the impact of Négritude on Richard Wright and James Baldwin. Specifically, I
discuss how Wright's and Baldwin's reactions to remarks made by Senghor and Césaire in Paris in 1956 during the First International Congress
of Black Writers and Artists emphasize the difficulty of trying to find, in
writing, a point of mediation between two disparate worlds: the African and the African-American. A guiding question in this chapter is one
posed by Wright after Senghor's eloquent presentation on "L'Esprit de
la civilisation ou les lois de la culture négro-africaine." In an attempt to
find a common denominator between himself and the African delegates,
Wright asks, "How do I latch onto this African World?"

In chapter 3, I focus on the problems of subjectivity and identity implicit in Wright's rhetorical response to Senghor and on the problem of
autobiographical writing. My reading of Wright's *Black Boy* and Maya
Angelou's *I Know Why the Caged Bird Sings* is organized around the
notion that autobiography or "auto-writing" may be seen as a process of
self/other creation in which the "I" that seeks to establish itself as subject
is always preceded by desire. This desire may center on an absent (African) world, or, as in the case of Angelou, on the mother, who engages in
a kind of Freudian *fort-da* game throughout the text. Among the critical
and theoretical problems interrogated in this chapter is, "How does the
'I' contextualize itself as 'black' or 'female' in an already established racist
and phallogocentric symbolic order?"

Chapter 4 is an engagement with feminism as it is practiced among
feminist literary critics. While the chapter's title strongly suggests that
my concern is with black feminist literary critics, my approach is cross-
cultural and interdisciplinary. My concern in this chapter is whether
(black) feminist literary discourse, operating as it does under the illusion
that it is working in the interest of a universal (black) Sisterhood, can
effectively "speak" on behalf of women who remain beyond the parameters of the American academy.

In chapter 5, I take up the problem of defining a theory of criticism for
black writing with greater specificity and relate it to what I have defined
as a crisis in the critical readings of black literature. Through a close reading of Houston Baker's *Blues, Ideology, and Afro-American Literature* and
Henry Louis Gates, Jr.'s *The Signifying Monkey* I show how, in many respects, the theories these critics employ in response to the crisis only serve
to deepen it. I do not agree, however, that the problem with their theorizing has to do with a lack of social or political consciousness as some

writers and critics contend. On the contrary, I find the social and political very much intact in their work despite the complexity of their discourse and methods. What is at issue in this chapter is the way Baker and Gates have attempted a re-evaluation of the values that subtend African-American literature through a wholesale appropriation of theories and concepts from the very systems against which they claim to be working. I feel that these writers' theoretical claims are extensive. They each seek a new way of apprehending the being of black literature. But what they have in effect offered, despite the critics who rail against them, are interesting literary histories that have indeed shaken, but have not upset, the status quo. It is my hope that this study will help to enrich the multiplicity of the debate so that the being of literary blackness will perhaps emerge on its own.

In "Toward a Conclusion" I reflect on the concept of double-consciousness and its implications for a thoroughly modern black literature. I also raise the question of what (black) literary theory reveals or conceals about reading and writing—indeed—about the being of (black) literature itself.

1 The Souls of Black Folk: Reading Across the Color Line

> I reached up and took out a fat black book, *The Souls of Black Folk,* by W. E. B. Du Bois. I turned the pages. It spoke about a people in a valley. And they were black, and dispossessed, and denied. I skimmed through the pages, anxious to take it all in.
>
> —Peter Abrahams, *Tell Freedom*

W. E. B. Du Bois's *The Souls of Black Folk* is, for many writers and critics throughout the African diaspora, an instituting text for twentieth-century black literature written in English.[1] Politically and ideologically framed by what Du Bois perceived as the problem of the twentieth century—the problem of the color line—it posits a founding metaphor, that of the Veil, and a founding concept, *double-consciousness,* for an ontology of blackness upon which is grounded the Black American literary tradition. *The Souls of Black Folk* also posits an aesthetic that has greatly defined the parameters of the tradition. It is, as Robert B. Stepto writes in *From Behind the Veil,* "the first substantial immersion narrative in the tradition; with its publication, all of the prefiguring forms and tropes that will develop another literary period are finally on display."[2] It contrasts with the other works included in Stepto's typology of African-American narratives in that it is Du Bois rather than some external (white) voice who assumes responsibility for "authenticating" his tale.[3]

Stepto describes this process of authentication in narratives before *The Souls of Black Folk* as being "based at least as much on race as on fact"; that is, it was generally a white person who confirmed, in writing, that a narrative's questing heroic figure "was where he said he was." He writes that in *The Souls of Black Folk* Du Bois changes the process by assuming responsibility for authenticating his text and his existence. Moreover, his narrative "advances a new scientific standard for what constitutes authenticating evidence." It scientifically gathers empirical evidence from such literal and figurative fields as the Southern Black Belt to complete the authenticating tasks that were previously given over to white public opinion (Stepto 63).

Du Bois claims responsibility for *The Souls of Black Folk* in "The Forethought" when he appeals to his "Gentle Reader" to "receive my little book in all charity, studying my words with me, forgiving mistake and foible for sake of the faith and passion that is in me, and seeking the grain of truth hidden there."[4] But what Stepto fails to see, and this is a major flaw in *From Behind the Veil,* is that this kind of documentation or attestation does not imply what he feels is authorial control of the text. Du Bois is in control of the text only to the extent that he *does* develop a strategy for his writing: writing requires a strategy; he *does* order his writing in a certain way; he lays out the text's structure in "The Forethought." But the counterpart to writing is reading, and since reading and writing are events occurring in language they cannot be controlled. Language itself is uncontrollable. We cannot control language. If anything, it may control us. The history of the relationship between blacks and whites in the United States is replete with examples to support the Heideggerian claim that "language . . . leaves itself to our mere willing and cultivating as an instrument of domination over beings."[5]

Stepto's definition of *The Souls of Black Folk* as the "first substantial immersion narrative in the tradition" refers specifically to the African-American protagonist's "ritualized journey into a symbolic South." However, in my reading of the text, I will disclose that the writing *exceeds* the parameters of the tradition as it is defined by Stepto. *The Souls of Black Folk* is equally immersed in the European (German Idealism) and American philosophical traditions. This immersion is announced by the title of the first chapter: "Of Our Spiritual Strivings." The chapter itself is a revision of an 1897 *Atlantic Monthly* magazine article that Du Bois published under the title, "Strivings of the Negro People."

While "Of Our Spiritual Strivings" might very well make more pronounced Du Bois's racial self-identification than the more "detached" original title as Stepto contends,[6] this new title also invokes the philosophical systems of Herder, Fichte, and particularly Hegel. Considering the fact that Du Bois studied with William James and Josiah Royce at Harvard[7] and with Heinrich von Treitschke at the University of Berlin (which was in the midst of a "Hegelian revival" when he arrived), it is reasonable to assume that, like most late nineteenth-century New England intellectuals, Du Bois would have been fairly well acquainted with Hegel's major philosophical texts. (In fact, Du Bois makes specific references to Hegel and Hegelianism in Lectures XX, XXXI, XXXIX and the final lecture of his Philosophy IV notebook.[8]) The chapter itself, as Joel Williamson points out in "W. E. B. Du Bois as a Hegelian," is laden with words that were favored by Hegel. Words such as *consciousness, double-consciousness, strife, self,* and *spirit* all point to a Hegelian metaphysics of the self.[9] More importantly, through his very influential, and very Hegelian, formulation of the notion of *double-consciousness,* Du Bois inscribes himself—and the African-American literary tradition—into the discourses of Western European philosophy. He writes,

> After the Egyptian and Indian, the Greek and Roman, the Teuton and Mongolian, the Negro is a sort of seventh son, born with a veil, and gifted with second-sight in this American world,—a world which yields him no true self-consciousness, but only lets him see himself through the revelation of the other world. It is a peculiar sensation, this double-consciousness, this sense of always looking at one's self through the eyes of others, of measuring one's soul by the tape of a world that looks on in amused contempt and pity. One ever feels his twoness,—an American, a Negro; two souls, two thoughts, two unreconciled strivings; two warring ideals in one dark body, whose dogged strength alone keeps it from being torn asunder.
>
> The history of the American Negro is the history of this strife,— this longing to attain self-conscious manhood, to merge his double self into a better and truer self. (17)

This very famous passage also demonstrates that Du Bois contextualizes the particular—the sociological and psychological ramifications of American racism on Black Americans—in familiar Western universals. What Stepto refers to as his "sustained evocation of the spiritual world of a race" arises out of the language of metaphysics (Stepto 66). And with that evocation arises a philosophical problematic: that of the existence of consciousness itself.

By 1904 William James, whom Du Bois acknowledges as his "friend and guide to clear thinking,"[10] had begun to seriously question whether consciousness could exist once Kant, with his "transcendental ego," had undermined the soul and thrown off balance its bipolar relation with the body. In "Does 'Consciousness' Exist?" James argues that in rational and empiricist quarters alike, the spiritual principle of these "equipollent" or equivalent substances "attenuates itself to a thoroughly ghostly condition, being only a name for the fact that the 'content' of experi-

ence *is known*. It loses personal form and activity—these passing over to
the content—and becomes a bare *Bewusstheit* [awareness] or *Bewusstsein
überhaupt*, [consciousness in general] of which in its own right absolutely nothing can be said." James calls this condition an "estate of pure
diaphaneity" or transparency. It marks the point at which consciousness
risks disappearing altogether except as the name of a nonentity. Consequently, James, who admits his twenty-year distrust of it, refuses to grant
consciousness a place among philosophical first principles. He also accuses those who are unwilling to abandon it for the more current notion
of absolute experience of "clinging to a mere echo, the faint rumor left
behind by the disappearing 'soul' upon the air of philosophy" and calls
for it to be "openly and universally discarded": "For twenty years past I
have mistrusted 'consciousness' as an entity; for seven or eight years past
I have suggested its non-existence to my students, and tried to give them
its pragmatic equivalent in realities of experience. It seems to me that the
hour is ripe for it to be openly and universally discarded."[11]

Fortunately, by the time James got around to trying to persuade his
students that consciousness did not exist, Du Bois had moved on. Had
he been among a later group of students, Du Bois might have hesitated
to use what had become, at least for James, a contentious concept for his
eloquent philosophical reflection on one of the *effects* of the problem of
the color line: that "peculiar sensation" of being caught up in an intermi-
nable dualism between the subject and the object, the body and the soul.
In any event, since James insists that consciousness stands as a function
for knowing rather than a quality of being, it is to Hegel and the *Phenomenology of Spirit* that we must turn in order to more fully apprehend
the philosophical implications of Du Bois's "double-consciousness." But
before we proceed, it is worth noting that, in "Hegel and His Method,"
James comments on what is a major obstacle for anyone who tries to explain Hegel: his "perverse preference for the use of technical and logical
jargon" and a style of writing that obscures his otherwise easy to grasp
central vision or thought.

> But if Hegel's central thought is easy to catch, his abominable habits
> of speech make his application of it to details exceedingly difficult to
> follow. His passion for the slipshod in the way of sentences, his un-
> principled playing fast and loose with terms; his dreadful vocabulary,
> calling what completes a thing its 'negation,' for example; his system-
> atic refusal to let you know whether he is talking logic or physics or

psychology, his whole deliberately adopted policy of ambiguity and vagueness, in short: all these things make his present-day readers wish to tear their hair—or his—out in desperation.[12]

Keeping James's warning of what lies ahead in mind, I hope to spare us from any unnecessary tearing of hair (and gnashing of teeth) by simplifying Hegel's thought as much as I dare. Also, at certain crucial points in my summary, I have quoted rather than paraphrased because, like William James, I am aware that "the only thing that is certain is that whatever you may say of [Hegel's] procedure, some one will accuse you of misunderstanding it."[13]

For Hegel, consciousness is "explicitly the *notion* of itself. Hence it is something that goes beyond limits, and since these limits are its own, it is something that goes beyond itself."[14] His *Phenomenology of Spirit* charts the "succession of experiences through which consciousness passes" as it progresses toward and transcends its own limits (55). Those experiences include consciousness as perception, as sense-certainty, as understanding, and as self-consciousness. Du Bois's notion of double-consciousness seems to correspond to this latter experience, to consciousness as self-consciousness.

In the section of the *Phenomenology of Spirit* entitled "Self-Consciousness," Hegel discloses the doubleness or duality of consciousness *in itself*. This doubleness occurs in two *distinct moments*. In the principle *distinct moment* consciousness is self-consciousness as otherness, an *immediately superseded* difference which, however, *is not*. It does not have the form of *being*, but rather that of *a being*. In the second *distinct moment* consciousness unites with this difference in the following manner:

> With that first moment, self-consciousness is in the form of *consciousness*, and the whole expanse of the sensuous world is preserved for it, but at the same time only as connected with the second moment, the unity of self-consciousness with itself; and hence the sensuous world is for it an enduring existence which, however, is only *appearance*, or a difference which, *in itself*, is no difference. This antithesis of its appearance and its truth has, however, for its essence only the truth, viz. the unity of self-consciousness with itself; this unity must become essential to self-consciousness, i.e., self-consciousness is *Desire* in general. Consciousness, as self-consciousness, henceforth has a double object:

one is the immediate object, that of sense-certainty and perception, which however *for self-consciousness* has the character of a *negative* and the second, viz. *itself* which is the true *essence,* and is present in the first instance only as opposed to the first object. (105)

Philosophically, then, what Du Bois argues is being denied blacks, "true self-consciousness," is *in itself* double-consciousness. As such, it is both in a unity with and in opposition to consciousness. However, this mode of consciousness as self-consciousness is only one instance of the doubling of consciousness. The other instances occur in what Hegel refers to as the "lordship and bondage" relationship and in the "Unhappy Consciousness."

Hegel's lordship and bondage relationship provided an important paradigm for many of the pro-abolitionist debates of the St. Louis Hegelians, a group of immigrant German intellectuals who helped to introduce German philosophy into New England Transcendentalism.[15] In the "lordship and bondage" relationship, self-consciousness is both independent of and dependent on an *other.* It exists as self-consciousness only insofar as it is acknowledged as such by another self-consciousness which it must supersede. Only through this supersession of the other, of the independent being, can it "become certain of itself as the essential being; ... in so doing it proceeds to supersede its *own* self, for this other is itself" (111). This process of the supersession of the "ambiguous otherness" and the returning *into itself* of self-consciousness which, according to Hegel, "has been represented as the action of *one* self-consciousness," has

> the double significance of being both its own action and the action of the other as well. For the other is equally independent and self-contained, and there is nothing in it of which it is not itself the origin. The first does not have the object before it merely as it exists primarily for desire, but as something that has an independent existence of its own, which, therefore, it cannot utilize for its own purposes, if that object does not of its own accord do what the first does to it. Thus the movement is simply the double movement of the two self-consciousnesses. Each sees the *other* do the same as it does; each does itself what it demands of the other, and therefore also does what it does only in so far as the other does the same. Action by one side only would be useless because what is to happen can only be brought by both. (112)

But these two sides are not equal. They are, in fact, opposed to each other since one side is only *recognized* while the other is only *recognizing*. Consequently, the essence and absolute object of self-consciousness, the 'I' or individual, is in conflict with another individual, or "unessential, negatively characterized object" (113). The conflict arises over the question of the "truth of self-certainty" which, as we shall see, Du Bois raises in the chapter on Alexander Crummell. For Hegel, each individual is

> certain of its own self, but not of the other, and therefore its own self-certainty still has no truth. For it would have truth only if its own being-for-self had confronted it as an independent object, or, what is the same thing, if the object had presented itself as this pure self-certainty. But according to the Notion of recognition that is possible only when each is for the other what the other is for it, only when each in its own self through its own action, and again through the action of the other, achieves this pure abstraction of being-for-self. (113)

With the truth of self-certainty at stake, the two self-consciousnesses enter into a "life-and-death" struggle with each other. Each individual self-consciousness must struggle to rid itself of its "self-externality" or otherness; for it is only through such a struggle that their "certainty of being *for themselves*" can be raised to truth (114). However, since life is the "natural setting of consciousness," and death is the natural negation of it, the truth that is supposed to issue from this "life and death struggle" is negated by it. What emerges instead is an independent (lord) and a dependent (bondsman) consciousness.

The relationship between the lord and the bondsman is mediated by things. It is the lord's desire for the thing that makes the bondsman dependent on him, for the bondsman is the one who forms and gives permanence to it. In so doing, he also realizes himself as an "alienated existence" whose *being-for-self* is actualized only through the thing and the work he performs on it. His is, therefore, a servile consciousness and not yet a true self-consciousness since the lord is its essential reality. Only when the two "moments" of fear and service conjoin with his *"formative activity"* does the bondsman's consciousness become a consciousness of itself as an essential being, "a being which *thinks* or is a free self-consciousness," and not something external to it (120).

This free and thinking self-consciousness sees itself as a being that *thinks* and holds something to be essentially important, or true and good only insofar as it *thinks* it to be such. It is, therefore, the consciousness of Stoicism, a thinking reality whose "aim is to be free, and to maintain that lifeless indifference which steadfastly withdraws from the bustle of existence, alike from being active as passive, into the simple essentiality of thought" (121). What it cannot withdraw from, however, is its otherness which manifests itself as Scepticism, a philosophical concept that gets considerable attention in the first five lectures of Du Bois's philosophy notebook.

It is in Scepticism that consciousness gets to know itself as a dual or double-consciousness, a consciousness containing contradiction within itself. This consciousness contrasts with the consciousness of Stoicism in that it negates the other consciousness even as it realizes it as one of its two modes of self-consciousness. Hegel describes this process of negation in the following passage:

> In Stoicism, self-consciousness is the simple freedom of itself. In Scepticism, this freedom becomes a reality, negates the other side of determinate existence, but really duplicates *itself*, and now knows itself to be a duality. Consequently, the duplication which formerly was divided between two individuals, the lord and the bondsman, is now lodged in one. The duplication of self-consciousness within itself, which is essential in the Notion of Spirit, is thus here before us, but not yet in its unity: the *Unhappy Consciousness* is the consciousness of self as a dual-natured, merely contradictory being. (126)

Contradictoriness is therefore the essence of the unhappy consciousness. It is essentially a consciousness "divided and at variance with itself," yet it is always striving for a reconciliation of the very elements that constitute its essence. Hegel continues:

> This *unhappy, inwardly disrupted* consciousness, since its essentially contradictory nature is for it a *single* consciousness, must for ever have present in the one consciousness the other also; and thus it is driven out of each in turn in the very moment when it imagines it has successfully attained to a peaceful unity with the other. Its true return into itself, or its reconciliation with itself will, however, display the Notion of Spirit that has become a living Spirit, and has achieved an actual existence, because it already possesses as a single undivided consciousness a dual nature. The Unhappy Consciousness itself *is* the gazing of one self-consciousness into another, and itself *is* both, and the unity

of both is also its essential nature. But it is not as yet explicitly aware that this is its essential nature, or that it is the unity of both. (126)

Du Bois's "double-consciousness" decontextualizes Hegel's "Unhappy Consciousness." That is, it creates a rupture between this particular technical term or "sign" and its historical and traditional context—German Idealism in all of its manifestations—and opens it up to other contexts. In this case, the new context is one upon which is inscribed the problem of the twentieth century: the problem of the color line. Hegel's "Unhappy Consciousness" is therefore *re*-contextualized into a problematic that is sociological, psychological, and philosophical, since, according to Hegel, consciousness, if it exists at all, is always a double-consciousness. It is always seeking to reconcile itself with its Other. It is always striving for "true self-consciousness." Therefore, in this philosophical paradigm, the Otherness with which the Negro seeks to reconcile himself is one of the elements that constitutes his essence as a social and psychological being. As the hyphenated nomenclature *African-American* implies, one of the Negro's two points of reference is America. The Negro, Black American, Afro-American, African-American is an American. As such, the "other world that looks on in amused contempt and pity" is, in fact, the Negro's world. And the irreconcilability of the Negro with that world is an essential part of the Negro's being-in-the-world.

While "Of Our Spiritual Strivings" is sociological, psychological, and philosophical (it implicitly invokes the philosophers and systems whose propositions form the structure of all of modern Western philosophy and its presuppositions), the second, third, fifth, sixth, eighth, and ninth chapters of *The Souls of Black Folk* tend toward a sociological investigation of the problem of the color line and its attendant problems, that is, Reconstruction, "Negro" leadership (chapter 3 is a critique of Booker T. Washington) and the education and training of black youth. In these chapters Du Bois lays out the scientifically gathered "empirical evidence" that Stepto claims constitutes a "new narrative mode and form." In chapter 6, for example, Du Bois responds to critics of higher education for blacks by presenting data from an Atlanta University survey about the more than 2500 blacks who by 1900 had earned Bachelor's degrees. About two-thirds of the graduates contacted responded to the survey. Over 53 percent of them indicated that they had pursued careers in education; 17 percent were theologians; another 17 percent were physicians or other "professionals;" 6 percent were merchants, farmers, and artisans; and 4 percent were employed in the government civil service (83). This evidence proved that, given the opportunity, blacks could "receive that higher training, the end of which is culture," and make significant contributions to the development of American civilization. And it is in the interest of culture that Du Bois asks, "What place in the future development of the South ought the Negro College and college-bred man to occupy" (84)?

Du Bois insists that technical and vocational training, while certainly necessary in a highly industrialized society, are not enough. They do not reach deeply enough into the "foundations of knowledge" and therefore cannot provide the kind of training and culture necessary to develop thinking men. One of Du Bois's two imperatives for the Negro College is that it "must develop men." The other imperative, stated less explicitly, has to do with the soul: "there must come a loftier respect for the sovereign human soul that seeks to know itself and the world about it; that seeks a freedom for expansion and self-development; that will love and hate and labor in its own way, untrammeled alike by old and new. Such souls aforetime have inspired and guided worlds, and if we be not wholly bewitched by our Rhinegold, they shall again" (87).

This second imperative echoes the German Idealist notion of the sovereignty of the human soul, and the Socratic ethical challenge to *know thyself*. Du Bois repeats this ethical challenge when he writes in "Of Alexander Crummell," "This is the history of a human heart,—the tale of a black boy who many long years ago began to struggle with life that he might know the world and know himself" (157). He also posits an Arnoldian concept of culture by calling for the development of great (black) men of culture who will prevail over and make current everywhere "the best that has been thought and known in the world."[16] Du Bois's imperatives are therefore moral and ethical. As such, they cannot *exceed* the discourse of metaphysics. Instead they combine with his empiricism to produce what Robert Stepto calls the "scholarly narrative posture or radical of presentation" that completes his "self-initiated authentication" (Stepto 63).

As a mode of authenticating or interpreting one's existence, this narrative posture must operate in what philosophy calls the "fore-structure" of understanding. It must proceed from a prior understanding of the world and what it means to be-in-the-world since, according to Martin Heidegger, "any interpretation which is to contribute understanding, must already have understood what is to be interpreted."[17] The movement of understanding and interpretation/authentication that structures Du Bois's "scholarly narrative posture" as Stepto describes it, is circular. Its circular movement traps Du Bois within the philosophical hermeneutic circle. However, as Heidegger writes in *Being and Time*, "What is decisive is not to get out of the circle but to come into it the right way," for hidden in the hermeneutic circle is "a positive possibility of the most primordial kind of knowing."[18]

What Du Bois seems to want to uncover from beneath the deep structures of racial oppression is the possibility for this kind of knowing. The desire for this "most primordial kind of knowing" sends Du Bois and his "weary travelers," Alexander Crummell in chapter 12, and John Jones in chapter 13, deep into the Southern Black Belt.

Du Bois develops his own Black Belt experiences in the fourth and seventh chapters. But while one is a slightly veiled autobiographical sketch, the other is characteristic of what Stepto refers to as an "immersion narrative." It records a mythical journey deep into the recesses of the Black Belt and into a historical epoch marked by two events: the great world-wide demand for cotton, and the systematic enslavement and exploitation of several millions of black people.

"Of the Black Belt" reverses one of the dominant themes of early African-American literature: the symbolic journey to the North and to freedom. This descent into the Black Belt *describes* a symbolic space that would later become very important for writers like Jean Toomer, Zora Neale Hurston, and Toni Morrison, among others. It is the Deep South after Emancipation—Albany, Georgia: a transitional society, a degenerating society—where Cotton was once king. Debt is now King Cotton's successor, for the booming cotton industry of the 1850s became a financial disaster in the 1880s; and where there was once opulence there now stands poverty and decay.

As our voyager makes his way through the Black Belt he observes that

wherever the King may be, the parks and palaces of the Cotton Kingdom have not wholly disappeared. We plunge even now into great groves of oak and towering pine, with an undergrowth of myrtle and shrubbery. This was the "home-house" of the Thompsons,—slave-barons who drove their coach and four in the merry past. All is silence now, and ashes, and tangled weeds. The owner put his whole fortune into the rising cotton industry of the fifties, and with the falling prices of the eighties he packed up and stole away. Yonder is another grove, with unkempt lawn, great magnolias, and grassgrown paths. The Big House stands in half-ruin, its great front door staring blankly at the street, and the back part grotesquely restored for its black tenant. A shabby, well-built Negro he is, unlucky and irresolute. He digs hard to pay rent to the white girl who owns the remnant of the place. She married a policeman, and lives in Savannah. (93)

Through the use of metaphor, which for Derrida is a "classic philosopheme, a metaphysical concept," Du Bois "negates" the *un*-sayable history of chattel slavery. In its place are *figured* the metaphors King/palace/Cotton Kingdom. These metaphors are "symmetrically opposed" to the properties that constitute the empirical reality of the slave system: Master/slave/slave-plantation.[19] Slavery is figured, or brought into presence, through the image of an aristocracy in decline. But that presence is only glimpsed. It is partially *veiled* by Du Bois's rhetoric which must rely on a "classical Aristotelian metaphor by analogy" in order to articulate the realities of a burgeoning industrial world.

In the preface to the 1953 Jubilee edition of his text, Du Bois makes the important point that when he wrote *The Souls of Black Folk*, he had not yet realized the influence of Freud or Marx, whose impact on the modern world he calls "tremendous." Therefore, in order to adequately represent the structures of the institution of slavery, he had no recourse but to draw analogies between it and the European aristocracy. But, in the interest of literariness, this analogy distorts the historical facts of slavery. Cotton *is not* king; slaveowners *are not* "barons"; and the cotton-growing South *is not* a kingdom. What *is* brought more clearly into presence is the fact that slavery has yielded to another form of labor: that of the black tenant farmer which, in many respects, is nothing more than slavery under a different guise since the tenant is perpetually endebted to his white landlord/lady. From one farm to another the situation is virtually the same. The black farmers can barely eke out a living for themselves. Those who do manage to see a profit are regularly cheated out of it. It is no wonder, then, that the blacks who greet the traveler form a composite picture whose dominating feature is despair.

Yet it is in this black peasantry, totally disenfranchised, that Du Bois believes the *spirit* of (Afro) American culture resides. This premise strongly influenced the writers of the Harlem Renaissance and the Black Arts movement and is, like the notion of double-consciousness, grounded in German Idealism.[20] Du Bois reiterates Herder, whose writings on the

German folksong (Volkslieder) not only influenced the internationalistic trend of the German folklore movement of the nineteenth century but also contributed to the building of a national German literature.[21] Indeed, the title of Du Bois's text itself, *The Souls of Black Folk,* re-marks and reiterates the two concepts—soul and folk—(Volk) that are central, not only to Herder's aesthetics, but to that of Hegel as well.[22]

Like Hegel, Du Bois sees the (black) "peasant" or slave in a relationship with nature that has been left intact by industrialism. He writes that "like all primitive folk, the slave stood near to Nature's heart" (186). In Hegelian terms, the slave shared with other peasant cultures a trust that "what it has put into the ground will come up of itself."[23] As the provider of crude labor, this peasant culture is likewise the locus of the Absolute trust that the state requires. And since this culture is not required to bring understanding into play with the command to provide crude labor, understanding is similarly brought into play in another domain: that of the harvest festivities, the folk songs, maxims, and lore it uses to sustain itself against the force that commands it to provide and to which it must obey.[24] Following Herder, Du Bois argues that this music, poetry, and dance unite a nation's folk-heritage and is the bulwark of nationalism. But for Du Bois, the music, poetry, and dance of the black folk are of great political and social significance. They challenge the popular belief that blacks have contributed nothing to the development of American culture. Du Bois urges black and white writers alike to preserve this folk heritage by working it into the structure of the nation's imaginative literature.

Aside from the harvest festivities, folk songs, maxims and lore that constitute the domain for understanding to be brought into play by the (black) peasantry, there is yet another domain: that of religion, or Christianity. This domain has perhaps more directly and profoundly influenced the development of a unique black folk culture than any other. In chapter 10 of *The Souls of Black Folk,* Du Bois discusses the role of religion, identifying three characteristics that typify the "religion of the slave": 1) the preacher, whom he calls the "most unique personality developed by the Negro on American soil"; 2) the music (which he discusses in greater detail in chapter 14); and 3) the frenzy which varies in expression "from the silent rapt countenance or the low murmur and moan to the mad abandon of physical fervor,—the stamping, shrieking, and shouting, the rushing to and fro and wild waving of arms" (141). Indeed, this "scene of human passion" and complete abandon is central to black folk culture. It is also arguably the least eurocentric domain of the culture. Traces of Africa are strongly inscribed upon this ritual of the Southern Baptist folk religion. And with the exception of death, it is the only instance that opens itself up to the possibility for transcendence, which is what the black "peasants" seek through their participation in the ritual: to somehow transcend the narrow and racially drawn confines of their (worldly) existence.

Death and transcendence are the "themes" of chapters 11 and 12. In chapter 11 Du Bois employs the language and rhetoric of romanticism to eulogize the death of his first-born child. Born within the shadow of the Veil, the child is destined to live a "living death." But Death—the "wraith of Life"—"jealously" intervenes, leaving the grieving father to wonder why he has been deprived of his "one little coign of happiness" within the shadow of the Veil:

> I am no coward, to shrink before the rugged rush of the storm, nor even to quail before the awful shadow of the Veil. But hearken, O Death! Is not this my life hard enough,—is not that dull land that stretches its sneering web about me cold enough,—is not all the world beyond these four little walls pitiless enough, but that thou must needs enter here,—thou, O Death? About my head the thundering storm beat like a heartless voice, and the crazy forest pulsed with the curses of the weak; but what cared I, within my home beside my wife and baby boy? Wast thou so jealous of one little coign of happiness that thou must needs enter there,—thou, O Death? (154–55)

But it is through death that the child transcends the world within the shadow of the Veil. In death the child, "if he still be," dwells "above the Veil."

Alexander Crummell, whom Du Bois eulogizes in chapter 12, also dwells above the Veil; but his mode of transcendence is based on knowing. Crummell exemplifies Du Bois's ideal of "book-learning" as the path "leading to heights high enough to overlook life" (19). However, this path is not without its racially inspired obstacles. The first abolition school Crummell attends is demolished by irate farmers; the theological seminary to which he applies refuses to accept 'Negroes'; and when he finally gets his own chapel, lack of participation among his black parishioners forces him to close. But Crummell strives on. Guided by the ethical challenge to "know thyself," Crummell desires to pass beyond the limits of "book-learning" into the realm of the knowable in order to ground for himself his own *self-certitude*. Crummell (and perhaps Du Bois), is therefore also guided by the Cartesian *Cogito ergo sum*.

The "hero" of chapter 13 is the antithesis of Alexander Crummell, yet he is guided by the same desire to know. Du Bois describes the "fictional" John Jones as a young man who spent his time "peering through and beyond the world of men into a world of thought" (169). His mode of thinking, however, is initially epistemological: why is a circle not square; why does this Greek word mean this and not that, and so on? What he learns is that there is no relation between this kind of knowledge—academic literacy—and freedom. The myth of the quest for literacy *and* freedom is nothing more than a myth for John Jones. After having spent seven years in his "queer thought-world," and having completed the symbolic journey to the North and the mythic freedom of the "World" of New York City, Jones returns to his native Altamaha only to find social conditions there intolerable. The white world insists that he conform to their codes of decorum and deference. The black world urges him to obey. And they both agree that the good boy, the "fine-plough" hand who was "handy everywhere and always good-natured and respectful" had been ruined (167). His death by a lynch mob is therefore the inevitable outcome of an aborted journey through literacy to freedom.

What remains "unspoken" in this and in chapter 12 is that both Crummell and Jones (and perhaps Du Bois) seek to move beyond the realm of finite knowledge and into that of infinite knowledge. The striving for this kind of knowing is, for Du Bois, characteristic of an epoch in which philosophy seemed to suddenly bring into sharp focus the dichotomy between the subject (the self) and the object (the world). In "Of Alexander Crummell" Du Bois describes this dichotomy as the primary metaphysical problematic of the nineteenth century:

> The nineteenth was the first century of human sympathy,—the age when half wonderingly we began to descry in others that transfigured spark of divinity which we call Myself; when clodhoppers and peasants, and tramps and thieves, and millionaires and—sometimes— Negroes, became throbbing souls whose warm pulsing life touched us so nearly that we half gasped with surprise, crying, "Thou too! Hast Thou seen Sorrow and the dull waters of Hopelessness? Hast Thou known Life?" And then all helplessly we peered into those Other-worlds, and wailed, "O World of Worlds, how shall man make you one?" (159)

The desire for a completion of the self in the other is one of the stable meanings of *The Souls of Black Folk*. However, under the dominance of the theme of the text—the problem of the color line, this desire does not readily reveal itself as a philosophical problematic.[25] But like the notions of *consciousness, double-consciousness, spirit,* and *striving,* the subject/object dichotomy, as Du Bois articulates it, presents a mode of philosophizing that conjoins with the methodologies of the social sciences. The text itself is a hermeneutical enterprise that involves the application of philosophy to "an historical interpretation of race relations" and engages a multiplicity of texts, both literary and philosophical.[26]

That Du Bois's text evolves out of a multiplicity of texts is made explicit by the epigrams and musical bars from the Sorrow Songs that precede each of the fourteen chapters. Written by some of the most prominent (and a few obscure) nineteenth-century poets, the epigraphs are fragments of other texts whose "parergon"[27] or en-framing is constituted by the American and European traditions. These two traditions are in turn infiltrated by other traditions, particularly the Greek and Hebraic traditions. The epigraphs and fragments from the Sorrow Songs therefore implicitly rupture the parameters drawn around *The Souls of Black Folk* by (black) literary criticism. The task of the critic, especially one who proceeds in the direction of Derridean deconstruction, is to demonstrate that implicitness. This is what Houston Baker forgets when he insists that the Sorrow Songs *displace* or *deconstruct* what he calls Western expressive culture: "if you look structurally at Du Bois's text, what you see at the beginning of every chapter is what would now be called, of course, a displacement or a deconstruction of Western expressive culture by the spirituals. Alright, I mean he will put Swinburne up there at the top, and then right under it comes the spiritual; I mean it wipes out Swinburne and Byron."[28]

The movements of deconstruction do not consist in simply opposing one mode of expression with another or in privileging one over the other as Baker does here. On the contrary, they refuse to give anything a privileged status. Furthermore, what they seek, ultimately, is a *dismantling* of the structure of Western philosophy and its presuppositions because, according to Derrida, structures always imply ideology, and ideology always brings interpretation to a close. In this sense, then, Derridean deconstruction would intervene in Western expressive culture in order to reflect on it since, lest we forget, its readings "must always aim at a certain relationship, unperceived by the writer, between what he commands and what he does not command of the patterns of the language that he uses. This relationship is not a certain quantitative distribution of shadow and light, of weakness or of force, but a signifying structure that critical reading should *produce.*"[29]

There is no such intervention by the Spirituals. Neither do they produce the kind of signifying structure Derrida says critical readings should produce. They can't because, as Du Bois is aware, the Spirituals are very much a part of Western expressive culture. By juxtaposing the bars from the Sorrow Songs with the poetic epigraphs, Du Bois does not displace or deconstruct the latter as Houston Baker contends. He merely *foregrounds* the very complex system of interrelationships that makes up his (con)textual field.

In the last chapter of *The Souls of Black Folk,* Du Bois discusses the importance of the musical bars. Some of them are from what he refers to as "master songs"—ten Negro folk songs or spirituals that have retained the rhythms of "primitive" African music. The others mark three stages in the development of Black American music: 1) the African songs that were imported from Africa by the newly arrived slaves; 2) the Afro-American field hollers and chants, into which the African rhythms eventually evolved, and 3) the blending of the Afro-American with "the music heard in the foster land" (184). This last stage is important in terms of Du Bois's *aesthetics* because it illustrates what he insists is the reciprocal relationship between the two cultures: "The result is still distinctively Negro and the method of blending original, but the elements are both Negro and Caucasian. One might go further and find a fourth step in this development, where the songs of white America have been distinctively influenced by the slave songs or have incorporated whole phrases of Negro melody" (185).

Du Bois does not deny, however, that certain breaches or ruptures occurred during this latter stage of the devolution of Afro-American music.[30] He writes that "words and music have lost each other and new and cant phrases of a dimly understood theology have displaced the older sentiment." He also accuses "conventional theology" and "unmeaning rhapsody" of having concealed the "real poetry and meaning" of the Negro songs (186). While he does not explain what the "older sentiment" was, or what constitutes "real poetry and meaning," it is interesting to note that Du Bois, whom Henry Louis Gates, Jr., quite accurately identifies as "probably the very first systematic literary and cultural theorist in the tradition,"[31] indicts what has been most influential in the development of the tradition: conventional theology. For as we shall see in the chapters devoted to feminism and Black American literary criticism and theory, it is theology or onto-theology[32] disguised under the rubric "criticism" that dictates what works shall and shall not be admitted into the canons of the feminist and Black American literary traditions.

In any event, Du Bois's position vis-à-vis the integral relationship between words (poetry) and music is a reminder that for many preliterate western and nonwestern societies, including that of the early Greeks, poetry was intended to be sung. Du Bois's complaint, like that of Plato, is that in the western tradition the voice—the words—have become subordinate to something else. For Plato that something else was instrumental effects; for Du Bois, as we have seen, it is a "dimly understood theology." In short, in this and in many other instances in *The Souls of Black Folk,* and in his writings on blacks and art, Du Bois is guided by the Platonism of the modern world historical situation. Consequently, he does not in any way displace or "deconstruct" Western expressive culture. He participates in it fully. In fact, Du Bois *positions* himself somewhere between the Western literary and philosophical registers when he writes at the end of "Of the Training of Black Men," "I sit with Shakespeare and he winces not. Across the color line I move arm in arm with Balzac and Dumas, where smiling men and welcoming women glide in gilded halls. From out the caves of evening that swing between the strong-limbed earth and the tracery of the stars, I summon Aristotle and Aurelius and what soul I will, and they come all graciously with no scorn nor condescension. So, wed with Truth, I dwell above the Veil" (87).

To sit with Shakespeare, to move with Balzac and Dumas, and to summon Aristotle and Aurelius is to inscribe oneself, implicitly, into a bound—*less* literal and figurative field of texts, subtexts, and intertexts. *The Souls of Black Folk* has expanded and enriched that field by raising the Veil that for too long has obscured from view a profoundly philosophical aspect of the problem of the color line. It also firmly secures Du Bois within the context of nineteenth-century New England intellectualism and as the first African-American philosopher of (double) consciousness. But Du Bois's influence extended beyond the borders of the continental United States. As we shall see in the next chapter, Du Bois had a profound impact on a group of young black intellectuals from throughout the African diaspora who, by the early 1930s, had gathered together in Paris in the name of black francophone Négritude.

2 Reading/Writing Négritude: Léopold Senghor and Aimé Césaire

Senghor (in Europe rootless and lonely) sings in art—lines
  of Black Woman.
Senghor sighs and, "negritude" needing,
speaks for others, for brothers. Alfred can tell of
Poet, and muller, and President of Senegal, who
in voice and body
loves sun,
listens
to the rich pound in and beneath the black feet of Africa.

—Gwendolyn Brooks, *In the Mecca*

In *Liberté 3: Négritude et civilisation de l'universel*,[1] the Sene-
gelese poet-philosopher-statesman Léopold Senghor pays tribute to Du
Bois and thereby establishes him as a founding father of one of the most
influential literary movements of the African diaspora: black francophone
Négritude. Senghor writes that it was Du Bois who first thought the
problem of Négritude, which is fundamentally a problem of identity, in
all of its complexities. He quotes a few lines from Du Bois's famous passage on double-consciousness to support his assertion that in order to
understand the basic premises of Négritude, Du Bois and *The Souls of
Black Folk* are the points from which one must always begin.

Senghor describes Du Bois's objectives and methodology as a two-part
process. The first has to do with erasing from the minds of whites *and*
blacks the image of the "degenerate black child" (*Nègre-enfant-taré*), and
substituting it with one from an authentic "classical" and self-sufficient
African civilization. The objective is to promote a desire in Black Americans to model themselves according to this new image of Africans. The
next step is to do away with racial discrimination, that is, all of the

constraints—economic, political, cultural, and social—that have reduced blacks to the status of second-class citizens. As Senghor puts it, "In short, it is a question of both an internal and external transformation of the American Negro. Internally, through education and training; externally, by an increasingly strong pressure exerted on public opinion and on the American government" (*Liberté 3,* 275). As we shall see, Senghor and the Martinican poet Aimé Césaire shared Du Bois's objectives. Their aim was to effect a similar transformation for all diaspora blacks. Like Du Bois, they both sought the creation of a new (black) human subject to replace the (white) image of the black as a "Nègre-enfant-taré." This transformation or (re)definition of the black subject was to be carried out primarily through objective forms of cultural production. Central to this (re)definition, for African-Americans and for "*les Nègro-africains,*" was a recovery, reconstitution, and (re)affirmation of the history and culture of the peoples of African descent. But these aims and objectives were articulated through the complex discourses of philosophy and the human sciences. In this chapter, I will specify the similarities and differences between Du Bois, Senghor, and Césaire and draw out the significance and implications of their discourses for an emergent criticism and theory specific to literary texts written by blacks.

In "Problèmatique de la Négritude," Senghor poses two questions that are crucial, both to Du Bois's notion of "double-consciousness," and to Négritude as an organizing concept for the category of blackness: "1) Does there exist, for blacks, specific problems based on the single fact that they have black skin or that they belong to an ethnic group which is different from that of the white and the yellow races? 2) What are these problems and under what circumstances are they raised" (*Liberté 3,* 269)? We have seen how Du Bois responds to the first question through his formulation of the notion of "double-consciousness" and how he presents the problems—as they affect African-Americans—through the theories and practices of the social sciences. But for Négritude and its practitioners the term *Négritude* itself is an important part of the problematic.

Senghor tries to resolve the problem by appealing to the laws of grammar (Senghor has complete and absolute faith in *French* grammar). In response to critics who have attacked Aimé Césaire for using the word *Négritude* instead of *Négrité* to convey the idea of blackness, Senghor argues that the suffixes *-ité* and *-itude* (from the Latin *-itas* and *-itudo*) convey the same meaning and that when Césaire coined the word he followed the most orthodox rules of the French language *(Liberté 3,* 269). Négritude therefore takes as its model the French word/concept *latinité*. Senghor refers to the *Petit Robert* definition of *latinité* to prove his point that *Négritude* is a perfectly legitimate term according to the French lexicon. "The *Petit Robert* defines the word latinité as follows: '1) way of writing or speaking Latin. Latin character; 2) (1835) the Latin world, Latin civilization. *The spirit of Latinity.*' According to this model, we could very well define Négritude as a 'way of expressing onself as a black person. Black character. The black world, black civilization'" (*Liberté 3,* 269).

The notion of *latinité* is a fundamental authority for Négritude's systematic thematic closure. Its grammar and logic are tools that work in the interest of establishing the limits of Négritude. They fix the norms for the elaboration of concepts and theories of blackness—concepts and theories appropriated primarily from the ethnography of Leo Frobenius—by which Négritude identifies itself and presents itself as what it is.[2] Négritude as a mode of philosophical reflection therefore takes epistemology as its point of departure.

The German ethnographer Leo Frobenius marks an important intersection between Du Bois, who often referred to his work in his own writings about Africa, and Senghor and Césaire.[3] It is through Frobenius's categories of ethnography that the latter two arrive where the former began: with German philosophy and Hegel. Senghor began to study Frobenius and ethnography in Paris at the Institute of Ethnography (*Liberté 3,* 13). This led him to "rediscover" the German philosophers, especially Hegel, Marx, and Engels whose works Senghor began to devour after his incarceration in a German POW camp.[4]

In "Négritude et Germanité" Senghor explains that the German *Wirklichkeitssinn* (sense of reality) is what impressed him most about German philosophy and inspired him after his discharge in 1942 from the POW camp to renew his acquaintance with its major philosophers. "'If . . . I again immersed myself in the German philosophers, beginning with Marx, Engels and Hegel; if after Sartre, I discovered Heidegger, it's undoubtedly because I felt, even among the socialist thinkers, that *Wirklichkeitssinn* which is the mark of German genius. Whether he observes matter or life, the fact or the phenomenon, even if he refuses it a priori, the German philosopher cannot resist going beyond the physical, into the *metaphysical*'" (*Liberté 3,* 16). Senghor says much the same thing in "Négritude et Germanité II." However, what he stresses in those remarks is that as he pursued the course he had outlined for himself, he ended up where he thought he should have begun—with Hegel: "after my discharge and demobilization in 1942, I again immersed myself in the German philosophers, beginning with Marx and Engels in order to end up where I should have begun: with Hegel to whom I added Husserl and Heidegger upon the advice of our compatriot, the philosopher Gaston Berger" (*Liberté 3*, 342). And in "La Négritude est accordée au XXème siècle," Senghor writes, "The paleontologists and ethnographers had proven to us that it is by relying on the natural environment, by reacting upon it, that man has moved away from animality. First Hegel, and then Marx and Engels presented man as having been produced by his own generic activity" (*Liberté 3*, 237).

Senghor was initially similarly attracted to Frobenius because he felt that the German ethnographer was the first to present a theory of the origin of culture and civilization that was compatible with Négritude as it was articulated in the 1940s. Like Césaire and the other Négritude poets, Senghor considered Frobenius's *Histoire de la civilisation africaine* and *Le Destin des civilisations* as "sacred" texts (*Liberté 3*, 13).

In these works, Frobenius argues persuasively that all cultures or civilizations, including African civilization, arise from the shock or *saisissement* experienced by man upon his contact with the real. According to Senghor, Frobenius calls this experience *païdeuma*. Senghor explains that *païdeuma*, as he understands Frobenius's use of the term, has to do with man's capacity to respond emotionally to the essence of things in such a way that it penetrates into his *conscience païdeumatique* or "cultural soul"[5] and acquires a new form as it passes from emotion to speech and finally to myth and idea. Emotion is crucial to Frobenius's concept of culture. Thus it comes as no surprise that the Négritude writers and poets felt that Frobenius, by strongly emphasizing the importance of emotion in the development of culture, had called into question popular European beliefs about Africa's lack of culture and civilization.

Frobenius had also called into question the traditional Western priority of discursive over intuitive reason. This is important, for as Senghor points out in "Les Leçons de Léo Frobénius," before encountering Frobenius who "clarified for [them] such words as *emotion, art, myth,* and *Eurafrique,*" the young blacks of the Quartier Latin were taught by instructors who, following the Cartesian method, insisted that they were to always allow themselves to be guided only by discursive reason—by fact, not feeling (*Liberté 3*, 399). In contrast, Frobenius had argued against this "dogmatic belief in the value of scientific knowledge," to borrow a phrase from Michel Foucault,[6] and its dominion over thinking in the modern Western world.

In *Le Destin des civilisations* Frobenius writes, "What we call civilization is often the expression of the soul, the language of the soul, at least when it has to do with men, whose thinking is still and especially *intuitive*."[7] This was an important lesson for Senghor who insists that "it is Frobenius who, more than all the others, more than Bergson, even, redeemed in our eyes intuitive reason and restored it to its place: to first place. After him we undertook a rereading of the philosophers and discovered that the Greeks granted priority to intuitive reason and that Descartes himself considered 'feeling' as one of the aspects of reason" (*Liberté 3,* 400). For Senghor, Césaire, and the other "Négritudists," this restoration of the primacy of emotion and intuition over discursive reason was essential to their struggle to recover their ethnic and cultural identity. Indeed, Négritude cannot be thought without the category of intuition and the notion that there exists a recoverable *original* "Negro-African" culture (*la culture négro-africain*).

In "Qu'est-ce que la négritude?" Senghor defines Négritude as "the totality of the values of the civilization of the black world as it is expressed in the life and the works of black people" (*Liberté 3,* 90). The notion of an original civilization whose originality is constituted by the Negro-African as natural man (*l'homme de la nature*) is central to Senghor's articulation of Négritude as a philosophical problematic. Following Frobenius's formulation of the binary opposition between discursive and intuitive reason and between the domains of factual and real phenomena, Senghor argues that what distinguishes the "negro-africain" from the European white is his mode of reasoning.[8] He writes that the former is guided by what he considers the basis of negro-african ontology: *intuitive reason,* while the latter's mode of reasoning is *discursive.* In other words, the European brings his analytical skills to bear upon a given object in order to take control of it. In so doing he never goes beyond mere appearances. The black man, through the power of his emotions, feels the object before it is bodily given and is therefore able to go beyond mere appearance to grasp the deeper reality for which the object is only a symbol (*Liberté 3,* 92).

By recasting Frobenius's binary, discursive/intuitive reason into a cultural-historical context specific to the Negro-African, and by emphasizing the idea of the object and the notion of a recoverable origin as organizing concepts for his philosophical system—indeed, by thinking

Négritude based on models provided by the concept of *latinité* and by ethnography, Senghor raises a phenomenological problematic that Négritude, because of its own ontological limits, is unable to address. For what is at issue in Négritude as Senghor articulates it is the role of the "Negro" subject/perceiver in the immediate apprehension of psychic and physical phenomena. Senghor insists that the black man feels (*Il sent*, from the verb *sentir*) the object before he sees it; that is, the object is somehow *presupposed* before it is bodily given, or represented. His theory raises yet another set of philosophical problems: the problems of *objectification, representation* (the privileged domain of everything that is), and *intentionality,* or the intentional acts—attention, will, desire, love, judgment, and so on—by which all lived experiences and all psychic comportment address themselves to what is.[9] These three categories help to determine the structure of intuitive reason which, let us not forget, is the basis of Senghor's Negro-African ontology.

According to Husserl, who by the mid-1940s had been added along with Heidegger to Senghor's list of contemporary German philosophers, intuition has to do with our "immediate perception of what is concrete" and is intrinsic to all human beings. Husserl refers to intuition as the "*essentially* naïve natural attitude" by which "human being" is "intentionally" directed toward the world and posits it (the world) as existing "without questioning the meaning of this existence and of the 'fact of its being given.'"[10] The fact of the existence of the world is "apodictically evident" or absolutely indubitable.

Concrete life as the object of intuition is not constituted by "purely theoretical representations" or objects as sets of physical properties, however. Intentions, which are themselves representations, are also constitutive of concrete life. As Emmanuel Levinas puts it in his interpretation of Husserl's theory of intuition, the world of action, beauty, ugliness, meanness, will, and desire all constitute the existence of the world and its rich structures in the same measure as such purely theoretical representations or categories as spatiality: "Will, desire, etc., are intentions which, along with representations, constitute the existence of the world. They are not elements of consciousness void of all relation to objects. Because of this, the existence of the world has a rich structure which differs in each different domain."[11]

Senghor, by positioning himself (and Négritude) as he does, confronts a problem that faces any form of philosophical reflection: namely the in-adequacy of philosophical language to represent the rich structures of the world's existence or to recapture a lost experience or origin. Reflection represents a specific eurocentric or methodological concept that belongs to a tradition (a textual or conceptual "field") *beyond* which the Négritude writers are trying to reach. Their quest for *noir*-ness is, fundamentally, a quest for a more original African (Césaire argues for a more original Greek) *life-world* [12] or world of already lived experiences with all of its rich structures. But within the parameters of the tradition of reflection, indeed, within the parameters of the language of dialectics with which the discourse of Négritude is heavily invested—perhaps within language itself—there is no possibility of experiencing this world or its structures.[13] Language exists as an *event* in the human being's lived experience. Lan-guage is what establishes, by the mere act of naming things-in-the-world, a community between beings and the life-world. Therefore, in order to raise the question of the origin of that world, it would seem that one would have to step outside of language itself.

Similarly, reflection does not allow for a retrogression to something which is not present in any way. That which is not present, in this case the *origin* of the African life-world, may only construct itself in the very pro-cess of moving back outside traditional philosophical reflection. Senghor attempts such a de(con)structive gesture by accusing writing of impover-ishing the real, by locating *all* of African civilization beyond writing, and by seeking, albeit blindly, the principles of an African aesthetic in Hei-degger's notion of *logos*.

In his highly mediated reading of Heidegger, Senghor tries to estab-lish a link between the logos as the "foundation of being" and what he calls the "negro-african philosophy of the word":

Heidegger began with the verb *legein* [*sic,* to lay] and the noun *logos* in order to examine the respective but convergent evolution of their significations, especially the ones they had at the very beginnings of Greek thought. . . . *Legein* began by signifying "to lay out" [*étendre*] or "letting-lie-before-gathering" [*laisser-étendu-devant-rassemblé*], before signifying "to pre-sent" [*pré-senter*], "to dis-close" [*exposer*], "to say" [*dire*], whereas *logos* signified "thoughtful pose" [*pose recueillement*], or more explicitly, thought-made-manifest [*recueillement rendant mani-fest*], or better, "thought and apprehension of the being of being" [*re-cueillement et appréhension de l'être de l'étant'*]. We are not too far from the Negro-African philosophy of the word. For it also, as we have seen, to speak [*parler*] is to gather [*recueillir*] the vital force, the being of being beneath its rough outline in order to lay it out by giving it form, that is to say, existence. (*Liberté 3*, 234)

It should be noted here that Heidegger's notion of logos, as it is articulated in "Logos (Heraclitus, Fragment B, 50)"[14] and in *Being and Time*, is much more complicated than the way it is presented in Senghor's summary. Heidegger, in his discussion of phenomenology in *Being and Time*,[15] deals with the logos as one of the two components, "phenomenon" and "logos," that constitute the expression *phenomenology*. Phenomenon signifies *"that which shows itself in itself, the manifest"* (BT 51). It stands in a relationship with semblance; but like semblance, it must be distinguished from appearance, which is not a "showing-itself," but rather "the announcing-itself by something which does not show itself, but which announces itself through something which does show itself" (BT 52). Stated differently, although phenomena are never appearances, every appearance is dependent on phenomena. Consequently, appearance is often understood as phenomena.

The word *logos*, whose basic signification is *discourse*, is also interpreted as *judgment, concept, definition, ground*, or *relationship*. As discourse, logos means making "manifest what one is talking about in one's discourse." It "lets something be seen, namely, what the discourse is about." Both *phenomenon* and *logos* therefore involve showing or letting-be-seen. Phenomenology means, then, "to let that which shows itself be seen from itself in the very way in which it shows itself from itself" (BT 58). It differs from such expressions as theology, and so forth, in that it "neither designates the object of its researches, nor characterizes the subject-matter thus comprised. The word merely informs us of the '*how*' with which *what* is to be treated in this science gets exhibited and handled." (BT 59). The *what* in this case is the Being of entities whose meaning, which has been so "extensively covered up and forgotten," can only be approached phenomenologically. According to Heidegger, "only as phenomenology is ontology possible" (BT 60).

Senghor's reading of Heidegger places him back in the domain of metaphysical reflection. He blindly assumes that Heidegger—through his preoccupation with the relationship between (hu)man, Being, the *logos* and *poësis*—is engaged in a "modern universal humanism" with its emphasis upon the "role and action of Man in and upon the world" (*Liberté 3*,

237). To this form of humanism, Senghor argues, the Negro-African and Negro-African culture, in short Négritude, have already responded affirmatively, particularly in the arts. As an idea, philosophy, life, theory, practice, ethic (*une morale*), and art—as an "objective civilization,"[16]—a *humanism*—Négritude therefore takes as its object Man. Heidegger, on the other hand, is concerned with what humanism, as it is articulated in twentieth-century discourses, obscures from man: his *essence* and its relation to the *truth* of Being.

↫

In the "Letter on Humanism," Heidegger questions the very terms— logic, ethics, physics—indeed the term humanism itself, that Senghor gathers under the rubric Négritude. Heidegger strongly implies that these terms, dominated as they are by the demands of the market of public opinion, signal a movement away from philosophy as thinking to philosophy as an occupation in competition with other such occupations and "isms": "One no longer thinks, but one occupies oneself with 'philosophy.' In competition such occupations publicly present themselves as 'isms' and try to outdo each other. The domination achieved through such terminology does not just happen. It rests, especially in modern times, on the peculiar dictatorship of the public ("Letter" 273). The instrument of this domination is language, which, in the process of objectifying and making accessible to everybody everything that is, becomes impoverished. It thereby endangers man's essence. It leaves the truth of that essence unthought.

Heidegger's notion of humanism consists merely in reinstating man in the "nearness of Being," of bringing man back to his essence: "Thus *humanitas* remains the concern of such thought; for this is humanism: to reflect and to care that man be human and not un-human, 'inhuman,' i.e., outside of his essence. Yet, of what does the humanity of man consist? It rests in his essence" ("Letter" 274). Heidegger feels that in the modern world this essence has been determined by the Marxist acknowledgment of man as a social being whose natural needs are secured through material production and by the Christian conception of man as the "delimitation of *deitas*," the "child of God who hears in Christ the claim of the Father and accepts it" ("Letter" 275). But humanism as *humanitas* is first encountered during the Roman republic when the term signified the following distinction between the *homo humanus* and the *homo barbarus*:

The *homo humanus* is here the Roman who exalts and ennobles the Roman *virtus* by the "incorporation" of the *païdeia*, taken over from the Greeks. The Greeks are the Greeks of Hellenism, whose culture was taught in the philosophical schools. It is the *eruditio et institutio in bonas artes*. *Païdeia* so understood, is translated by *humanitas*. The authentic *romanitas* of the *homo humanus* consists of such *humanitas*. In Rome we encounter the first humanism. It, thus, remains in its essence a specific Roman phenomenon, born of the encounter between the Roman and Hellenistic cultures. ("Letter" 275)

All subsequent humanisms derive from this Roman *humanitas*. And while they differ in aims, doctrines, etc., they all "coincide in that the *humanitas* of the *homo humanus* is determined from the view of an already-established interpretation of nature, of history, of world, of the basis of the world (*Weltgrund*), i.e. of beings in their totality" ("Letter" 276). In accord with Heidegger, then, to think Négritude as a humanism is to further impede the questioning of the relation of Being to the essence of (the black) man. As a humanism in competition with the dominant European institutions of knowledge, Négritude does not allow for the possibility of thinking Negro-African culture in a new and original way. This kind of thinking requires that one move "away from the thin abstractions of representational thinking and the stratospheric constructions of scientific theorizing, and toward the full concreteness, the onefoldness of the manifold, of actual life-experience."[17] From a Heideggerian perspective, the only domain that opens up such a possibility is that of the poetic experience. But as we shall see, in Négritude that domain, like all its other constitutive domains, is dominated by the already established Western (German, French, Greek) interpretation of nature, the world, and beings in their totality.

The domain of the poetic experience is privileged in Négritude because, as Senghor points out in his reading of Heidegger, it is the domain where the *logos* stands in close proximity to beings and Being. But Senghor, *occupied* as he is with philosophy, can only explain the complex relation between the *logos,* beings, and Being in terms of its instrumentality. Heidegger on the other hand thinks of the relation as a "site" on which poetry and thinking are brought together. In *On the Way to Language* Heidegger writes that *logos* "speaks simultaneously as the name for

Being and for Saying" and is specifically directed toward what he calls the nearness or the "neighborhood of poetry and thinking."[18] The word *saying,* which is related to the Old Norse *saga,* means "to show, to make appear, the lighting-concealing-releasing offer of world" (*OWL* 107). It is the "guiding key word" to the nearness or "neighborhood" of poetry and thinking, themselves modes of Saying, which, in their "face-to-face" encounter with each other, open up the possibility for a *thinking* experience with language. This thinking experience offers no commonsense or practical wisdom, however. It is not a problem-solving enterprise. What it offers is the possibility of experiencing the essence or the "primal tidings of linguistic nature." What it draws us close to is *"The being of language: the language of being"* (*OWL* 94).

Language in this context is not thought of as a mere human faculty, a fact that Senghor overlooks in his appropriation of Heidegger. Heidegger writes that, in the Western metaphysical tradition, language as a human faculty is "represented as speech in the sense of vocal sounds" and is placed within the "metaphysically conceived confines of the sensuous" (*OWL* 97). From within these confines what remains to be questioned with regard to the being of language is, according to Heidegger, "whether the real nature of the sounds and tones of speech is thus ever experienced and kept before our eyes" or whether the technological and calculating perspective of physiology and physics keep us from *properly* considering the kinship between melody and rhythm and song and speech as an essential property of language (*OWL* 98). Hence, from this perspective, Senghor has not considered the matter "properly." In his attempt to place Negro-African culture 'beyond' writing, he appeals to the technological. In fact, he bases Négritude's "aesthetic dimension" and the privileged place occupied by poetry in that dimension on a "metaphysical-technological" explanation.

Senghor describes the Negro-African poet and his French counterpart as technicians. Like the mathematician with his variables, they are masters of their tools (*outils*), of language (*langue*) and of speech (*parole*). And they all have something to say. "The sculptor, the painter, the architect, indeed the musician, has, first of all, something to say. And he says it in his language which is a panoply of instruments, dictionary of signs, net for the miraculous draught of metaphors [*filet pour la pêche miraculeuse des métaphores*]" (*Liberté 3,* 25). Thus we arrive once again to what I referred to in chapter 1 as a "classic philosopheme" and "metaphysical concept," *metaphoricity.* We also arrive at an important juncture between the poetry and poetics of Négritude and that of continental France: the poet of signs, symbols and metaphoricity par excellence, Stéphane Mallarmé.

It might seem somewhat ironic that although Mallarmé is considered one of the nineteenth century's most obscure and inaccessible poets, the Négritude poets found much to admire in his work. According to Senghor, what attracted the Négritude poets to Mallarmé was his desire for a poetry that would liberate the word from any kind of function or instrumentality. In *Pour une lecture Négro-Africain de Mallarmé* he explains that nothing is more essentially black or Mallarméan than a poetics in which the word is not reduced to its primary function. Hence the point in which their thinking about poetry converges: "Here we touch on one of the underlying reasons for bringing Mallarmé and the black poets together. We are all striving, in a similar ontological design, to 'give a purer meaning to the words of the tribe:' to give them, through that purity, the power to invoke the hidden world."[19]

Mallarmé goes beyond this point, however. He tries to render all meaning impossible because he believes that only when language fails— when language means *nothing*—can lyric poetry, as an absolute idea, come to be. The mere possibility of lyric poetry, Mallarmé believes, rests upon the notion of nothingness or the void, a notion that Négritude, as a humanism and as a philosophy of presence, finds intolerable. What this all means is that while Senghor embraces Mallarmé and symbolism for their reaction against rationalist positivism and for the primacy they give to intuitive reason, he must also reject them on the grounds that what the Negro-African ultimately seeks in symbolism is not the "*idée pure*" or the abstract, but the concrete—the *beyond* as it is made manifest in each lived experience. Nevertheless, Senghor feels that because symbolism places so much emphasis on intuition, its impact on Négritude, as well as that of Mallarmé, cannot be overstated.[20] As Senghor puts it, "It's this primacy given to intuitive over discursive reason that explains, at the end of the 19th century, the encounter between Stéphane Mallarmé and Négritude."[21]

By the force of his argument about the primacy of intuitive over discursive reason, by his upholding of the ideal of intuition, which like objectivity, is grounded in the epistemological model of the Cartesian tradition, Senghor brings us full circle. We have come to the beginning point once again. But as we have already seen in the previous chapter on

Du Bois, what is at issue with regard to the hermeneutic circle is not its circularity, since circularity is what underlies and is presupposed by all understanding and interpretation. What remains to be asked is whether Senghor, through his logic and by dint of his having to pass through the beginning point again and again, makes of the hermeneutic circle a *circulus vitiosus*. On this question let us turn now toward Aimé Césaire.

Cercle non vicieux

Penser est trop bruyant
a trop de mains pousse trop de hannetons
Du reste je ne me suis jamais trompé
les hommes ne m'ont jamais déçu ils ont des regards qui
les débordent
La nature n'est pas compliquée
Toutes mes suppositions sont justes
Toutes mes implications fructueuses
Aucun cercle n'est vicieux
Creux
Il n'y a que mes genoux de noueux et qui s'enfoncent
pierreux
dans le travail
des autres et leur sommeil[22]

Nonvicious Circle

Thinking is too noisy
has too many hands grows too many cockchafers
Moreover I have never been wrong
men have never disappointed me they have looks which
transcend them
Nature is not complicated
All my assumptions are correct
All my implications fruitful
No circle is ever vicious
Hollow
It is just my knees which are knotty and sink
stonelike
into the labor
of others and their sleep[23]

"Aucun cercle n'est vicieux." This raises yet another question: why is no circle vicious? The poem seems to imply that, at least within the domain of the poetic experience, thinking, through its excessiveness, negates the conditions for establishing the necessary logical paradoxes by which the viciousness of the circle is generated.[24] This excessiveness is articulated through the first line of the poem, *"Penser est trop bruyant/*Thinking is too noisy," by the repetition in the second line of the adverb *trop* (too, too much, too many) and in the fifth line by the third person plural form of the verb *déborder* (to overflow, go beyond, surpass). This is not to suggest, however, that "Cercle non vicieux" does not establish itself in a logico-rhetorical manner. At a functional level, lines three through eight do precisely that. They affirm the correctness and productivity of all of the suppositions and implications of the "I" *before* positing it as an authority on circles. They invest the thinking/speaking subject with the power to make the claim that *"Aucune cercle n'est vicieux."*

Like Senghor or, for that matter, any writer engaged in developing strategies for interpreting what is, Césaire is also entrapped in the hermeneutic circle. But he enters it differently. Despite the by now well known fact that he was the first to use the term *Négritude* in an attempt to define the essence of blackness, Césaire is not as *occupied* as Senghor with Négritude, philosophy, and humanism. In fact, he rejects Négritude as an ideology and therefore opens it up to greater, and perhaps more "deconstructive" potentialities.

Césaire also rejects any theory of literature that places literature at the service of a politics. He therefore stands in opposition to critical and theoretical enterprises that attempt to develop standards for judging literary works based on prevailing dogmas. For example, Césaire once remarked to Lilyan Kesteloot that from a literary point of view and as a personal ethic, he accepts Négritude. But during his discussion with Kesteloot he made it clear that he was opposed to an ideology based on Négritude because he didn't believe that it or any theory of literature was of much value when placed at the service of a politics.[25]

Whether or not Césaire has since changed his attitude about the political value of literary theories is open to debate. Suffice it to say that, at least through the 1970s, when it comes to literature Césaire's primary concern seems to be with literature *as such*—with the relation between language, writing, poetry, thinking, and being—and the extent to which the domain of the poetic experience opens up the possibility of discovering the being of blackness. This is not to suggest that Senghor is any less talented, dedicated, or engaged a poet than Césaire, however. On that point, Senghor's poetry speaks for itself. But Senghor's poetry is in the interest of *some* thing, whether it be Négritude, universal humanism, or some form of nationalism; whereas Césaire's involvement with poetry is in the interest of the *disclosedness of being* (black). Since the *disclosedness of being* has no interest other than being as such, the concept of being does not run the risk of becoming an ideology. It simply places the poet in a very close proximity to thinking and to the "pure idea."

In a provocative article titled "Sur une poésie nationale," which was written in response to René Depestre's proposal for a national poetry for black people, Césaire argues against a poetry that does not just let poetry *be*. He writes that Depestre, whose "Un débat autour des conditions d'une poésie nationale chez les peuples noirs," is strongly influenced by Louis Aragon's essays on a national French poetry, has not presented the problem well.[26] Césaire feels that Depestre subverts his own intention by specifying Aragon's nationalism as a model for a national "Antillian" poetry. Césaire argues that Depestre is correct when he writes that "it would be a mistake on our part, a denial of nationalism, to ignore the African screen, [le *volet africain*] which figures at the window of our national traditions."[27] But Depestre contradicts himself by following Aragon, whose model renders subordinate everything that is not French or is not compatible with the French prosodical heritage (*l'héritage prosodique français*). (It should be noted that Senghor makes the same mistake, particularly in his essays on the virtues of the French language, French poetry, French culture, the French press, and just about everything else that can be called French.)

The problem, then, becomes one of grounds, for if Aragon's model is the best one for a national Antillian poetry as Depestre contends, the elements that constitute the African screen or *volet,* which the poet seeks to retain risk being rejected in the process of elimination he would be required to undergo in order to "harmoniously" integrate them into the French poetic tradition.[28] Césaire calls this a strange reversal of values and accuses Depestre of falling into a "detestable assimilationism."[29]

This kind of assimilationism presupposes a fixed form into which the poet need only recall his experience. It also posits a metaphor—"*mouler son inspiration.*" Césaire urges the poet to struggle against this kind of metaphor so that the poem, as a portion or "afflux" of life, may find or invent its own equilibrium. "It is decidely high time to react against this kind of metaphor. You say 'mouler son inspiration,' etc. . . . . etc. . . . the truth is totally different. A poem is a part of life, a flood of life which takes hold of sonorous reality and finds, invents for itself its own equilibrium."[30]

Césaire is equally opposed to the idea of an a priori fixed traditional European or African form capable of accommodating the experiences of the modern black poet. He argues that the latter can only result in exoticism, which, in his opinion, is as serious or grave a problem as assimilation. "To think that there is an African form into which the poem must fit at all costs, to think that it is a question, in this mold constituted in advance, of forcibly fitting into it our experience as modern black poets, seems to me the best way of running, this time not into assimilationism, but something no less serious, into exoticism."[31]

Thus, for Césaire, these borrowed forms are insufficient for a national poetry. He feels that for there to be a national poetry, one must let poetry be. (*Que la poésie soit—et c'est tout*). In order for a national poetry to be, its domain can only be circumscribed by the *authentic*, by the manner in which the poet comports himself toward the poem: "I think that if the poet commits himself in a way that is truly complete, his poetics, if he is African can be nothing other than an African poetics; that if the poem is good, if the poem comes from far enough away, it can only carry the poet's mark, his essential mark, that is to say, his national mark. Who, more than the poet, is of his time, his milieu, his people?"[32]

In "Poésie et connaissance," an essay that elaborates a kind of "criterion for pure poetry," Césaire implies that to commit oneself totally is to come to the poem with all of one's being, to saturate the poem that is to be (*le poème qui va se faire*) with the totality of one's lived experiences; in short, to cease to practice poetry (and perhaps, philosophy) as an occupation and to enter into the *adventure* of poetry.[33] Césaire feels that only when the poet and the poem have no other ambition than that of poetry itself, will the mark of nationality be inscribed upon them.

In what is perhaps his most strident remark about his own status as a national poet, Césaire rejects the very premises—the "isms" by which he has been identified—on the grounds that beyond marking solidarity among the most insulted people in history, they serve no aesthetic purpose. "They talk about my 'inspiration négriste,' my 'pan-négrisme,' etc. . . . This really makes no sense. To be aware of being black when one lives in a world infected with racism; to think that this consciousness imposes on those who have it, special tasks—such as solidarity with the most insulted people in history—in no way merits the pomp of some 'ism.'"[34]

Césaire concludes "Sur la poésie national" by arguing that black poets have nothing to gain by locking themselves in an aesthetic whose historical considerations are unclear simply because it responds to someone's personal tastes: the dialectics of an epoch do not amount to the whims of a privileged few. He also feels that Black poets are mature enough to run the risks of the *adventure* of freedom and to pay the price exacted by poetry and by revolution: "we are grown-up enough to run, at our risk and peril, the great adventure of Freedom; our poetry exists at the cost of our right to initiative, as well as our right to error. I'm thinking about poetry. And revolution also."[35]

The condition for poetry (and perhaps for revolution) as Césaire understands it is what he believes Mallarmé and the surrealists were able to effect through their violent attacks on the French language, that is, the complete failure of language itself. Mallarmé had achieved what Césaire says he had always tried to do: he "dislodged" the French language from its performative function by making it *inflective* rather than *reflective*. Césaire discusses the great influence Mallarmé had on him in an interview with Jacqueline Leiner:

> I have always wanted to *inflect* French. Thus, if I have really liked Mallarmé, it's because he showed me, because I understood through him, that language is, basically, arbitrary. This is not a natural phenomenon. That prodigious phrase that Mallarmé wrote: *"my instinct regrets that discourse fails. . . . Only, let us know that verse would never exist:* philosophically, it remunerates the defect of languages." . . . my effort has been to *inflect* French, to *transform* it in order to express, let us say, "this me, this me-negro, this me-creole, this me martinican, this me-antillais." That is why I am much more interested in poetry than in prose and the former *to the extent that it's the poet who creates his language.*[36]

Like Mallarmé, Césaire feels that he is remaking language. But he insists that this new language is *not* French: "I am remaking a language which is not French. If the French find themselves there, it's their problem!"[37] He feels that this new, inflective language and the mode of writing he adopted from the surrealists could help to "decolonize" the French language (and the black mind) by resisting the assimilationists and the dominant, eurocentric culture. And most importantly, it could help to conjure up, from the depths of the unconscious, not only that which is "fundamentally black" but that which can be called *true poetry*.[38]

Césaire explains to Jacqueline Leiner that for him, *true poetry* is subversive to the extent that it rises from out of the depths rather the surface of oneself.[39] True poetry is subversive (*boulversante*) because it takes language out of its role in everyday experience. In everyday experience, language as communication takes on an authoritative character: "Things are so because one says so."[40] This authoritative character of language therefore encourages an "undifferentiated kind of intelligibility" that "releases one from the task of genuinely understanding" the entities within-the-world by prescribing one's state-of-mind and determining what one thinks and how one sees.[41] Poetic language seeks to establish itself as a "counter-communication" in order to return language to what, in Heidegger's words, are the "primal tidings of linguistic nature," or what Césaire calls, in "Poésie et connaissance," its pure condition (*l'état pur*): "A pure condition. That is to say subject not to custom or belief, but to the unique urging of the cosmos. The poet's word, the primitive word: rupestral design in sonorous material."[42] In a poem entitled "Mot" (Word), Césaire shows how in everyday language the word, loaded as it is with signification, obstructs one's access to a genuine understanding of the nature of one's being-in-the-world:

Mot

   Parmi moi
de moi-même
à moi-même
hors toute constellation
en mes mains serré seulement
le rare hoquet d'un ultime spasme délirant
vibre mot
    j'aurai chance hors du labyrinth
plus long plus large vibre
en ondes de plus en plus serrées
en lasso où me prendre
en corde où me pendre
et que me clouent toutes les flèches
et leur curare le plus amer
au beau poteau-mitan des très fraîches étoiles

vibre
vibre essence même de l'ombre
en aile en gosier c'est à force de périr

le mot nègre
sorti tout armé du hurlement
d'une fleur vénéneuse
le mot nègre
tout pouacre de parasites
le mot nègre
tout plein de brigands qui rodent
des mères qui crient
d'enfants qui pleurent
le mot nègre
un gresillement de chairs qui brûlent
acre et de corne
le mot nègre
comme le soleil qui saigne de la griffe
sur le trottoir des nuages
le mot nègre
comme le dernier rire vêlé de l'innocence
entre les crocs du tigre
et comme le mot soleil est un claquement de balles
et comme le mot nuit un taffetas qu'on déchire
le mot nègre
        dru savez-vous
de tonnerre d'un été
          que s'arrogent
                des libertés incrédules

             Word
         Within me
from myself
to myself
outside any constellation
clenched in my hands only
the rare hiccup of an ultimate raving spasm
keep vibrating word
                I will have luck outside of the labyrinth
longer wider keep vibrating
in tighter and tighter waves
in a lasso to catch me
in a rope to hang me

and let me be nailed by all the arrows
and their bitterest curare
to the beautiful center stake of very cool stars

vibrate
vibrate you very essence of the dark
in a wing in a throat from so much perishing
the word nigger
emerged fully armed from the howling
of a poisonous flower
the word nigger
all filthy with parasites
the word nigger
loaded with roaming bandits
with screaming mothers
crying children
the word nigger
a sizzling of flesh and horny matter
burning, acrid
the word nigger
like the sun bleeding from its claws
onto the sidewalk of clouds
the word nigger
like the last laugh calved by innocence
between the tiger's fangs
and as the word sun is a ringing of bullets
and the word night a ripping of taffeta
the word nigger
     dense, right?
from the thunder of a summer
    appropriated by
        the incredulous liberties [43]

In the beginning the word is bound up with the "Moi" as a kind of primordial totality. Outside of any constellation except the one constituted by the "Moi," tightly clenched in its hands, the word does not vibrate. But that totality is ruptured in the sixth verse by the "rare hiccup." In the seventh verse the word begins to vibrate, perhaps creating the labyrinth in the eighth verse, outside of which the speaking subject will have luck.

The vibrating spreads in verse nine. And in verses ten through fifteen the vibrating word does violence to the speaking subject. Its waves "lasso and rope him to a vodun center stake where a shamanic sacrifice ensues:"[44] the curare on the arrow tips is emptied into him with all the bitterness of the howling, vibrating word. In lines sixteen and seventeen, the sacrificed speaking subject challenges the already vibrating word: "vibre/vibre essence même de l'ombre." The vibrating word responds by springing out, armed with its "howl" in all of its traditional, social, and historical implications, from the poisonous flower. This vibrating word is a signifying word: *nigger* (*nègre*), which as the last two lines of the poem affirm, arrogates to itself "incredulous liberties." Those "incredulous liberties" are what Césaire seeks to deprive the excessive and licentious vibrating/signifying word of so that poetry and perhaps Being (black) can be restored to a more pure condition. And it is to that end that Césaire, like Mallarmé, cultivates the "rare word" (*le mot rare*) and the tight syntactical structures characteristic of Mallarmé's sonnets.[45]

Let us take as an example of Césaire's pure or "true poetry" the poem titled, ironically perhaps, "Présence":

> tout un mai de cañeficiers
> sur la poitrine de pur hoquet
> d'une île adultère de site
> chair qui soit prise de soi-même vendange
> O lente entre les dacites
> pincée d'oiseaux qu'attise un vent
> ou passent fondues les chutes du temps
> la pur foison d'un rare miracle
> dans l'orage toujours crédule
> d'une saison non évasive

> Presence

> a whole May of canafistulas
> on the chest of pure hiccup
> of an island adulterous to its site
> flesh which having possessed itself harvests its grape self
> O slow among the dacites
> a pinch of birds fanned by a wind
> in which the cataracts of time pass blended

the sheer profusion of a rare miracle
in the ever credulous storm
of a nonevasive season [46]

In contrast to "Mot," which, despite its complexity, opens itself up to
interpretation through a vocabulary familiar to most readers of French
and through the repetition of the verb "vibrer" and the phrase "le mot
nègre," "Présence" is, at least for this reader, "hermetically sealed." It
does not "speak," as does "Mot," directly to a social or political problem.
Neither does it posit a kind of subjectivity. Like many of Césaire's poems,
"Présence" is "encrypted" by a lexicon derived in part from the flora
and fauna specific to equitorial Africa and the Antilles and by a syntax
heavily informed by what Césaire refers to as his Mallarméan side (*mon
coté mallarméen*). Its potential therefore does not lie in its referentiality.
"Présence" does not allow for an external vantage point. In Derridean
terms, "*il n'y a pas de hors-texte.*" "Présence" seems to refer to nothing outside of itself. What it seems to *present* is a self-contained universe whose
potential lies in its self-reflexivity and the extent to which it engages the
reader in the act of reading.

Reading is not to be understood here as simply the horizontal activity of following a line of writing or text, however. Recent theories
such as Formalism, Phenomenology, Hermeneutics, and Deconstruction
have show reading, as an endless, completely undetermined act, to be extremely problematic. But this problem we shall defer until we take up
the critical theories of Houston Baker and Henry Louis Gates, Jr. What
I wish to point out here is that "Présence," through its non-referentiality,
calls into question the notion that reading generates self-awareness. For
if "Présence" generates an awareness of anything, it is the indeterminate-
ness of language itself. "Présence," in its negation of presencing, releases
language from the word's bond with things and makes pure poetry and
the pure idea its only destination.

As Césaire makes clear in his interview with Jacqueline Leiner and elsewhere in his writings, much of his success as a poet is due to the great
influence that French poets like Rimbaud, Lautréamont, Mallarmé, and
the surrealists have had upon him. However, as Edward A. Jones recalls in "Afro-French Writers of the 1930s and the Creation of the *Négritude* School," when he met Césaire in 1935, the Martinican poet was also

"deeply immersed in the literature of the Black experience, especially in the United States," and included in his readings the works of Langston Hughes, Claude MacKay, Jean Toomer, and Sterling Brown's *Southern Road*.[47]

What I find curious is that, unlike Senghor who frequently comments on the impact these writers had upon his developing black consciousness, Césaire seems reluctant to discuss his relationship with them. For example, when Jacqueline Leiner asked him to talk about the black American poets in the interview that prefaces the 1978 edition of *Tropiques,* Césaire responds that he and his group had very little contact with them. Apparently, their limited finances prevented them from socializing with the Americans, although they did go out with Langston Hughes, Countee Cullen, and Claude MacKay, all of whom became their "personal baggage."[48] In this discussion and elsewhere, Césaire stresses the fact that the Afro-American writers played a minor role in his development as a poet and that the guiding key concepts for his aesthetics and his politics were derived primarily from French literature, Nietzschean philosophy, and the ethnography of Leo Frobenius. Nevertheless, in the July 1941 issue of *Tropiques,* Césaire did pay tribute to the black poets in "Introduction à la poésie nègre américaine," which is accompanied by French translations of James Weldon Johnson's "The Creation," Toomer's "Harvest Song," and Claude MacKay's "To America."

It would be difficult to speculate in retrospect on Césaire's reluctance to discuss his relationship with the Afro-American writers he met during the 1930s and 1940s. However, by 1956 when the "First Congress of Black Writers and Artists" was held in Paris, it was clear that there existed a certain degree of animosity between the two groups.[49] This animosity was brought out during a dispute initiated by Richard Wright over where American blacks stood in relation to the African world that Senghor had defined in his presentation to the audience that had packed into the Salle Descartes at the Sorbonne to witness this historic event.

After Senghor's elaborate presentation on "L'Esprit de la civilisation ou les lois de la culture négro-africaine," Richard Wright addressed the gathering in a language laced with irony:

I was stupefied with admiration with what Leopold Senghor said here today, and it is towards his remarks that I want to address myself. . . . It was a brilliant speech and a revelation to me—a brilliance poured out in impeccable, limpid French, about the mentality and sensibility

of the African;—a poetic world, rich, dynamic, moving, tactile, ryth-
mic. Yet, as I admired it, a sense of uneasiness developed in me. . . .
I wonder where do *I*, an American Negro, conditioned by the harsh
industrial, abstract force of the Western world that has used stern,
political prejudices against the society (which he has so brilliantly elu-
cidated)—where do *I* stand in relation to that culture?[50]

Wright told the audience that everything he has ever written or said had
been in deference to that culture, but he implied that blackness was not
sufficient for him to accept Africa, which he suspected as having been
complicit in its own colonization, as *his* world: "Where do I latch onto
this African world? Is it possible for me to find a working and organic
relationship with it?"[51] Césaire offered an indirect response to Wright's
question in his opening remarks of "Culture and Colonization" by establishing the colonial situation as the common denominator for all blacks,
including American blacks whose subject position in a modern racist
society could only be understood as a form of colonialism.[52]

   According to A. James Arnold, while Césaire's Marxist analysis in
"Culture and Colonization" provoked an "explosion of joy" among the
other delegates, the Americans were outraged by Césaire's characteriza-
tion of them as a colonized people.[53] The deeply offended John Davis
defended the United States by arguing that every American president
from Washington to Dwight Eisenhower had always taken an anticolo-
nialist position.[54] But a cable from Du Bois explaining why he could not
be present supported Césaire's contention that American Blacks are similarly colonized, thereby further straining the already tense relationship
between the five Americans and the other delegates.

   In "Princes and Powers" Baldwin describes the "great stir" caused by
Du Bois's cable, which began with "I am not present at your meeting
because the U.S. Government will not give me a passport," when it was
read to the packed Descartes amphitheater.

   The reading was interrupted at this point by great waves of laughter, by no means good-natured, and by a roar of applause, which,
as it clearly could not have been intended for the State Department,
was intended to express admiration for Du Bois' plain speaking. "*Any
American Negro traveling abroad today must either not care about Negroes
or say what the State Department wishes him to say.*" This, of course, drew
more applause. It also very neatly compromised whatever effectiveness

the five-man American delegation then sitting in the hall might have hoped to have.[55]

But Baldwin's interpretation is not altogether accurate. What Du Bois in fact wrote was that "Any Negro-American who travels abroad today must either not discuss race conditions in the United States or say the sort of thing which our state Department wishes the world to believe."[56] The primary target of Du Bois's attack was not the American delegation,[57] as Baldwin's interpretation of the cable seems to suggest, but rather the United States government's very undemocratic practice of depriving certain of its citizens of their basic civil rights, not the least of which is the right to free speech.[58] Nevertheless, as Ambroise Kom points out in his discussion of the 1956 Congress, what the message implied was that the American delegates were agents of the Department of State.[59] In any event, Baldwin, echoing Richard Wright, calls into question one of the basic premises of Négritude and its competing epistemologies: that there exists an African life-world common to all black people in the world.

Baldwin writes that after the morning session, when Wright introduced him to the other members of the American delegation, he momentarily found it quite unbelievable (ludicrous, perhaps?) that they were being *defined*, indeed, that they had been brought together by their relation to the African continent, a relationship that for them had yet to be clarified. But as Baldwin was well aware, that relationship could not be made clear until the problem of the question around which the Congress was organized, "What *is* a culture?" was somehow resolved. Baldwin writes that under the most serene circumstances, this would be a difficult question, and that in the context of the conference, it was one that "was helplessly at the mercy of another question: Is it possible to describe as a culture what may simply be, after all, a history of oppression? . . . For what, beyond the fact that all black men at one time or another left Africa, or have remained there, do they really have in common?"[60] However, as the debate went on it became apparent to Baldwin that, despite their "widely dissimilar experiences," what all black people shared was "their unutterable painful relation to the white world. What they held in common was the necessity to remake the world in their own image, to impose this image on the world, and no longer be controlled by the vision of the world and of themselves, held by other people. What, in sum, black men held in common was their ache to come into the world as men."[61]

But from what, or from where does this image of their own making derive? Ignoring the cultural context to which the individual black writer owes his identity, Senghor argues that it derives from his African heritage. To support his argument, he discusses what he calls the African tensions and symbols with which Wright's poem "I Have Seen Black Hands" and his autobiography, *Black Boy*, are involved, but about which Wright is unaware.[62] Baldwin finds Senghor's position rather tenuous, however, since in his opinion, *Black Boy* owes its existence to factors that relate specifically to the experiences of a "Negro boy in the Deep South." Baldwin feels that "in so handsomely presenting Wright with his African heritage, Senghor seemed to be taking away his identity" as an American Negro.[63] He explains that he has always thought of *Black Boy* as a major American autobiography, and that although there might be something African in it just as there is "undoubtedly something African in all Negroes," the question of what that something is and how it has survived remains open. Moreover, Baldwin argues, the fact that it was written in the English language further complicates the problem of where the text stands in relation to the African heritage as Senghor defines it.

> *Black Boy* had been written in the English language which Americans had inherited from England, that is, if you like, from Greece and Rome; its form, psychology, moral attitude, preoccupations, in short, its cultural validity, were due to forces which had nothing to do with Africa. Or was it simply that we had been rendered unable to recognize Africa in it? —for it seemed that in Senghor's vast re-creation of the world, the footfall of the African would prove to have covered more territory than the footfall of the Roman.[64]

This position brings us back to Wright's question. Constrained as he is by the authority of the Western literary tradition, but invested with what Du Bois calls a "double-consciousness," and which Wright, reiterating Du Bois, refers to as a double vision and an organically born racial identity that stems from one's being a product of Western civilization, or more particularly, the American South, "Where do I [the African-American writer] latch onto this African world?"[65]

This question forces me to ask: how is it possible to recreate, in the English, French, or Spanish languages and through cultural practices modeled on European modes of cultural exchange, this world whose history or "image" has already been repeatedly *dissimulated* through several hundred years of "vivid and bloody" writing? Moreover, how is the similarly constrained critic to render recognizable whatever African elements inhabit the black text without first establishing a "working and organic relationship" with that world? Is it possible to establish such a relationship through the discursive practices of Négritude or the Black Aesthetic, or for that matter, the "New" Black Criticism of Baker, Gates, and Stepto? Or is Richard Wright correct in implying that in relation to Senghor's African world, the American Negro signifies the *Other?* These questions are no less complex than the one that guided the 1956 Congress of Black Artists and Writers and will be dealt with more fully in chapter 5. What I would like to turn our attention to now is how the themes of double consciousness and of Otherness are developed in Wright's *Black Boy* and in another major American autobiography, Maya Angelou's *I Know Why The Caged Bird Sings.*

3 The Auto-Text: On Inscripting Otherness; or Alas, Poor Richard, Poor Maya

[George Lamming] found . . . something crippling in the obsession from which Negroes suffered as regards the existence and the attitudes of the Other—this Other being everyone who was not Negro.

—James Baldwin, *Nobody Knows My Name*

Otherness has become the great obsession of late twentieth-century literary studies. This development can be attributed in part to the influence of psychoanalysis, particularly the work of Jacques Lacan, which sees literature as a kind of test site for its theories of the unconscious as the "discourse of the other." No less influential, especially for those who have been relegated to the margins of society (and of critical discourse), is Du Bois's notion of "double-consciousness." In chapter 1 I showed how this double-consciousness derives from Hegel's discussion of consciousness, self-consciousness, and otherness in the *Phenomenology of Spirit*. Lacan's notion of Otherness likewise derives in part from Hegel and from his radical re-reading, through the language of structural linguistics, of Freud whose influence Du Bois had not yet felt when he published *The Souls of Black Folk*.[1] Therefore, what remains undeveloped in Du Bois's formulation of double-consciousness is the role played by desire in the intersubjectivity of the Negro and the Other: the desire for reconciliation with that "other world" that looks on in such "amused contempt and pity"; Richard's desire to latch onto an African world that might exist only in the rhetoric of Négritude, and onto the "something different" of the world of Western literature; and Maya's desire for the always absent mother in Maya Angelou's *I Know Why the Caged Bird Sings*.

In any event, as Blacks, Women, Gays, Lesbians, and everyone else who is likely to fall under the rubric Other were admitted into the "Court of Western Literature," mainly through the different area studies that have become institutionalized over the past two decades, Otherness became a new center from which they would demand a fair hearing. What they demanded was a *space* within the institution from which they could articulate their diversity or difference. In other words, the Other sought to constitute itself, from *within* the already established racist and *phallogocentric* symbolic order, as the subject of its own discourse. In the Afro-American literary tradition, that demand was often most strongly articulated through the autobiographical statements of its writers, as recent critical and theoretical works on Afro-American autobiographical writing have shown. In fact, some critics—Joanne Braxton and James Olney come most immediately to mind—have argued that the current popularity of autobiographical writing in American literary studies in general can be directly attributed to the political upheavals of the 1960s. The turmoil and unrest that forced the Academy to reevaluate its position vis-à-vis the Other also created what Braxton in *Black Women Writing Autobiography* calls an "improved publishing climate" that allowed more of those Other voices to be heard.

As the academy attempted to compensate for its benign neglect of the Other by introducing area studies programs, autobiography began to assume an important ideological function, as James Olney points out in *Autobiography: Essays Theoretical and Critical*. Olney writes that for certain newly developed area studies—for example, American Studies, Black Studies, Women's Studies, and African Studies—autobiography constitutes a kind of organizing center. He argues that it can therefore be seen as rendering "in a peculiarly direct and faithful way" the same experience and vision that underlies and informs all the literature of a given people.[2] The importance of this center for contemporary black women writers is underscored by Marjorie Pryse who, in her introduction to *Conjuring*, writes that the autobiographical writings and slave narratives of nineteenth-century black women writers "must be our starting point."[3] Thus far, Pryse's imperative has received its most complete articulation in Braxton's *Black Women Writing Autobiography*.

Black Women Writing Autobiography traces the development of the theme of the quest for a "self-defining identity" in the autobiographical writings of black women from Harriet Jacobs to Maya Angelou. Braxton relies on Erik Erikson's theories of adolescent ego identity formation and Albert Stone's *Autobiographical Occasions and Original Acts* to make her argument that for the women included in her study, autobiography was a "refuge" that allowed them to resolve whatever "identity confusion" they might have experienced as the result of American racism and sexism. What she fails to address adequately, however, is how this identity becomes "self-defining" in writing. This is important because one of Braxton's implied objectives in *Black Women Writing Autobiography* is to deepen the literary analysis of black women's autobiographical writing. Such a project would require going beyond the ideological functions of autobiography and dealing much more critically than Braxton (or, for that matter, Erikson or Stone) does with the problems of the *I,* the *subject,* the *voice,* and with autobiography's often ambiguous status as a literary genre that hovers somewhere between the "real" and the "fictive." As Paul de Man has shown in "Autobiography as De-facement," this ambiguity derives, in part, from the fact that "autobiography *seems* to depend on actual and potentially verifiable events in a less ambivalent way than does fiction. It *seems* to belong to a simpler mode of referentiality, of representation, and of diegesis."[4] He goes on to suggest that any deviations from reality—phantasms, dreams, and so on—retain their verisimilitude by remaining "rooted in a single subject whose identity is defined by the uncontested readability of his proper name."[5] In other words, we assume that autobiography is a product of the true and verifiable lived experiences of the subject whose proper name is inscribed on the cover of the book. Autobiography as a literary genre has traditionally announced itself in this way.

De Man questions this assumption by suggesting that autobiography might depend less on referentiality, that is, on the "actual and potentially verifiable events" that constitute a life, than on the technical demands of self-portraiture by which the writer engaged in the autobiographical project is governed. He asks,

> but can we not suggest, with equal justice, that the autobiographical project may itself produce and determine the life and that whatever the writer *does* is in fact governed by the technical demands of self-portraiture and thus determined, in all its aspects, by the resources of his medium? And since the mimesis here assumed to be operative is one mode of figuration among others, does the referent determine the figure, or is it the other way round: is the illusion of reference not a correlation of the structure of the figure, that is to say no longer clearly and simply a referent at all but something more akin to a fiction?[6]

To these questions Richard Wright and Maya Angelou, both of whom remain among the most widely read Afro-American autobiographers, would probably respond affirmatively. For neither of them ever forgets that they are *writers*. As such they, like other writers who take their craft seriously, are governed by the technical demands of their medium at least as much as they are by their lived experiences. One need only look at Wright's meditation on writing in "How Bigger Was Born" to see that he took most seriously the problems generated by the very act of writing. That he took no less seriously the act of writing his autobiography is obvious from his remark that "writing like this is a kind of war and revolution."[7]

Wright embarked upon his autobiographical project shortly after April 9, 1943, when he spoke to a packed audience at Fisk University about his experiences with racism while living in the South. Convinced after his less than enthusiastic reception that the problems of race had not been sufficiently explored because everyone tried to avoid them, Wright began stringing together his "autobiographical notes, thoughts, and memories" into a "running narrative" about how "one black boy grew up in the South."[8] However, as James Olney hastens to caution us, that "black boy" and Richard Wright are not one and the same. The "I" that "speaks" as Richard is not the same person as Richard Wright. They are separated, not only by the distance of many miles and more than thirty years, but by what Olney refers to as Wright's "encompassing and creative memory." This memory allows Wright to imagine into existence the central figure of *Black Boy* in much the same way he imagined into existence the figure of that other black boy, Bigger Thomas. It is also what joins the *bios,* the "course of the lifetime" of the "I" that is Richard in *Black Boy* with that of Richard Wright the "autobiographer."[9]

In *Black Women Writers at Work,* Angelou makes clear her commitment to writing when she says that her responsibility as a writer is to be as good at the craft of writing as she can be. "So I study my craft. I don't simply write what I feel, let it all hang out. That's baloney. That's no craft at all."[10] As a student of the craft of writing and as an autobiographer and poet, one of Angelou's struggles has been with maintaining sufficient distance from her lived experiences so that she can write about them. To that end, Angelou makes a distinction between the Maya character and herself: "Whenever I speak about the books, I always think in terms of the Maya character. . . . I would refer to the Maya character so as not to mean me."[11] Furthermore, although she considers all of her

major works to be autobiographies, Angelou insists that when she wrote
I Know Why the Caged Bird Sings, she was less concerned with her own
life or identity than with positing the Maya character as a central figure.
This figure was to be the focal point around which would be organized
the events that influenced the lives of a number of people during a particular time—during Angelou's childhood and adolescence—in order to
show how one person, Maya Angelou, survived that time.[12] In this sense,
then, the figure in *I Know Why the Caged Bird Sings,* like that of *Black Boy,*
does indeed "determine the referent." The "illusion of reference" is in fact
"a correlation of the structure of the figure, that is to say no longer clearly
and simply a referent at all, but something more akin to a fiction."[13]

In this context, then, the autobiographical project in *Black Boy* and
I Know Why the Caged Bird Sings can be seen as much more complex than
a "simple presentation of [black and gendered] identity." Indeed, the assumptions about the relationship between that identity and the empirical "I" are called into question, for as someone once put it, "I am one
thing, my writings are another matter."[14] Similarly Angelou, when asked
by Claudia Tate how she feels about her past works, responded, "Generally, I forget them. I'm totally free of them. They have their own life. . . .
The work, once completed, does not need me. The one I'm working on
needs my total concentration. The one that's finished doesn't belong to
me anymore. It belongs to itself."[15]

My reading in this chapter of Wright's *Black Boy* and *I Know Why the
Caged Bird Sings* is organized around the notion that "auto-writing," as
I shall call the autobiographical project, may be seen as a process of self/
other creation in which this figure, this "I" that seeks to establish itself as
the subject of its own discourse is always a displacement. Writing across
Lacanian discourse, I argue that this "subjectivity" signifies something
other than the signatory whose name is inscribed upon the text. And it
is always preceded by a desire for that which is never present. As I have
already stated, this desire may center on an absent world, or as in the case
of Maya, the inaccessible mother, which the writing engages in a kind of
Freudian *Fort-da* game throughout the text. But since this desire is much
deeper, greater, and more primordial than need, it can never be fulfilled.

&

If we were to concede that everything that is not Negro is Other, as
James Baldwin suggests in the epigraph that precedes this chapter, then
the Negro could not be the Other. But the identity of the Negro as Negro

is predicated upon this Other, as Du Bois has shown. To restate this in Lacanian terms and by analogy, in Du Bois's formulation of double-consciousness, the first object of desire of the Negro as Other is to be recognized by the other (world).[16] Therefore, within what Lacan calls the Symbolic Order, the Negro as Other is always *subjected* to its *intersubjective* Other, as my reading of *Black Boy* and *I Know Why the Caged Bird Sings* will show. But first, to establish a relation between the Lacanian other and otherness as it is generally understood in Afro-American literary discourse, I must make a brief detour into the domain of Lacan's Symbolic Order.

In Lacan, the Symbolic is one of three registers or orders. The others are the Imaginary and the Real.[17] The Symbolic is a pre-established human order that structures all relationships, including the relationship between the self and the other. This order, which is only realized in language as such, is constituted by a network of symbols or "signifiers" that Lacan claims is so total that it joins together, prior to birth and unto death and beyond, the shape of one's destiny (*Ecrits* 68). In other words, this network "fixes" such categories as the human and the social.

Within this network or "chain of signifiers," Lacan has erected the Phallus as the primary signifier. However, as Jacqueline Rose remarks in her translation of Lacan's *Feminine Sexuality,* the phallus is not to be understood here as that which marks the biological difference between the sexes, but rather as a signifier for the law of the father.[18] Lacan, in "The Meaning of the Phallus," stresses this point. He writes that for him the "relation of the subject to the phallus is set up regardless of the anatomical difference between the sexes" (*FS* 76). It should be noted, however, that Lacan also stresses the fact that he does not argue for "man's relation to the signifier as such" from a "culturalist" position. His concern is with rediscovering, in the laws governing the unconscious, "the effects discovered [by Freud] at the level of the materially unstable elements which constitute the chain of language: effects determined by the double play of combination and substitution in the signifier, along the two axes of metaphor and metonymy which generate the signified; effects which are determinant in the institution of the subject" (*FS* 79).

Despite Lacan's anticulturalist position, his "rediscovery" of these effects can provide insight into the institution, in writing, of the subject as a color-coded and gendered entity. For as Juliet Mitchell explains in her introduction to *Feminine Sexuality,* Lacan's work challenges the Humanist belief that "man is at the centre of his own history and of himself" and that "he is a subject more or less in control of his own actions, exercising choice" (FS 4). She argues that Lacan shows instead that the human animal is born into language and comes into being as a human subject from within the construct of language as such. "Language does not arise from within the individual, it is always out there in the world outside. . . . Language always 'belongs' to another person. The human subject is created from a general law that comes to it from outside itself and through the speech of other people, though this speech in its turn must relate to the general law" (FS 5).

Lacan, following Lévi-Strauss, describes this general law as predicated on the primordial law of the father and the prohibition of incest. He describes the law as "that which in regulating marriage ties superimposes the kingdom of culture on that of a nature abandoned to the law of mating. The prohibition of incest is merely its subjective pivot, revealed by the modern tendency to reduce to the mother and the sister the objects forbidden to the subject's choice, although full license outside of these is not yet entirely open" (Ecrits 66). Ironically, one of the earliest extant sets of written laws governing marriage ties, property rights, and the prohibition of incest, the Hammurabi Code, is engraved on a phallic shaped stone object which is 7'6" high, 5'4" in circumference at the top, and 6'2" in circumference at the bottom. One could say that Lacan's primary signifier receives its most complete objectification in this big black thing which the Louvre museum in Paris considers one of its great treasures.[19]

Lest we forget, however, Lacan defines the paternal law in relation to the practice of psychoanalysis. His concern is with how the name of the father, as it is encrypted within this primordial law, affects the outcome of the psychoanalytic experience: "It is in the *name of the father* that we must recognize the support of the symbolic function which, from the dawn of history, has identified his person with the figure of the law. This conception enables us to distinguish clearly, in the analysis of a case, the unconscious effects of the function from the narcissistic relations, or even from the real relations that the subject sustains with the image and the action of the person who embodies it" (Ecrits 67).

Considering the fact that Lacan's critical paradigm is the unconscious as it is represented in speech during psychoanalysis, and that within this paradigm the phallus *as primary signifier* is privileged while the mother and daughter are reduced to objects that are "forbidden to the subject's choice," I, like Hortense Spillers, must pause for a moment to ponder the appropriateness of applying such a paradigm to Afro-American auto-

biography (or fiction) where the historical fact of American slavery and its residuals are always present.[20] In her essay on the incestuous link between fathers and daughters in Ralph Ellison's *Invisible Man* and Alice Walker's "Child Who Favored Daughter," Spillers reminds us that American slavery "permitted none of the traditional rights of consanguinity."[21] The American slave codes dictated that the offspring of a female slave would always follow her condition but would never belong to her. Thus, the "maternal prerogative" that was assured those *Other* mothers would never be hers, while the African-American father was, as Spillers puts it, "figuratively banished"—prohibited from entering that "social fiction" called fatherhood without the "behest" of someone else.[22] The "African person" was, therefore, figuratively (and often literally) "twice fathered," a person that "could not be claimed by the one and would not be claimed by the other," a "social subject in abeyance," a "new synthesis" engaged in a "fatal play of literally misplaced/displaced names."[23]

In *Black Boy* this drama of the "misplaced/displaced names" is played out in the following exchange between Richard and his mother:

> "What was Granny's name before she married Grandpa?"
> "Bolden."
> "Who gave her that name?"
> "The white man who owned her."
> "She was a slave?"
> "Yes."
> "And Bolden was the name of Granny's father?"
> "Granny doesn't know who her father was."
> "So they just gave her any name?"
> "They gave her a name; that's all I know."
> "Couldn't Granny find out who her father was?"
> "For what, silly?"
> "So she could know."
> "Know for what?"
> "Just to know."
> "But for *what*?"
> I could not say. I could not get anywhere.
> "Mama, where did Father get his name?"
> "From his father."
> "And where did the father of my father get his name?"
> "Like Granny got hers. From a white man."
> "Do they know who he is?"
> "I don't know."
> "Why don't they find out?"
> "For what?" my mother demanded harshly.
> And I could think of no rational or practical reason why my father should try to find out who his father's father was. (57)

Perhaps there is no rational or practical reason beyond Richard's desire to establish his patrilineage. For what Spillers calls "the line of inheritance from a male parent to a female [or male] child"[24] seems to have been effectively severed by the written and unwritten codes that have traditionally protected the name of the white father while guaranteeing his right to give his slaves—his children—a name. But Wright's rendering of his protagonist's frustrating inquiry into the origin of Granny's name reinforces, if only "by accident,"[25] Lacan's ideas about the general law of the father and its correlate, phallic signification, since even during slavery all familial relations, no matter how tenuous, were literally shaped and governed by the law of the often unnamed and absent (white) father. And it is against this father's (un)name that Richard, at least implicitly, seeks to identify himself. Granny's mother's name is not important in this exchange; neither is the name of Richard's father's mother, or his father's father's mother. In this sense, then, "the kingdom of culture" does indeed prevail over nature, or as Ellie Ragland-Sullivan rephrases it in "Seeking the Third Term," it's "father's name over mother's body."[26]

In "Seeking the Third Term," Ragland-Sullivan attempts to establish a first cause for what she refers to as masculine violence and aggression and the role that language as a *living material* plays in spurring individuals to violence and such "subject functions" as narcissistic aggrandizement, desire, love, and so on (60). She proceeds from what she calls the Lacanian view that "the problem for males . . . is that they are asked to identify away from the mother in the name of a father who is supposed to be an ideal (in the imaginary and symbolic), but is, in actuality, the source of prohibition" (40). Ragland-Sullivan sees this as a sort of double bind. It places the son in a "confused position in terms of both ego and desire." Unlike the daughter whose identification with the mother is encouraged and approved very early in her life, the son can be neither mother nor father. "He can only await from a posture of aggressive frustration the position of power tacitly promised" by the father's name (41). Ragland-Sullivan reads Lacan's phallic signifier as a social law that, in the symbolic order, "divides the subject from conscious knowledge of its own roots" in the materiality of language, that is, in the "inmixing of the imaginary and real" that gives language its "affective body:"

> In the symbolic order, the phallus stands for social law and is seen in
> many cultures as a structuring cause—an encounter with the real—of
> which subjects are effects. Between the symbolic and the real one meets
> cultural desire regarding the masculine and the feminine. Between the
> imaginary and the symbolic phallic effects are felt as prohibitive words,
> as a superego. In this sense the phallus is a third term that stakes out
> the structure of an ideal ego, as well as the limits of anxiety and the

causes of guilt. One could go farther and argue that the symbolic order is itself a third term that functions to smash imaginary fantasies and symbiotic collusions, opening the door to the play of retaliatory aggressivity in language, whether one refers to disagreements, derisions, or annihilative tactics. (63)

In short, Ragland-Sullivan sees the third term, be it the phallus or the symbolic order itself, as a defense mechanism against the prohibitiveness inherent in the name of the symbolic father. From this perspective, the kitten killing scene in *Black Boy* can be read as an acting out, in language, of Richard's unconscious desire to annihilate that which stands for the source of all of his prohibitions—his *real* father.

Richard first becomes aware of his father as a distinct personality when the family moves to Memphis, where they share a two-room apartment in a one-story brick tenement: "It was in this tenement that the personality of my father first came fully into the orbit of my concern. He worked as a night porter in a Beale Street drugstore and he became important and forbidding to me only when I learned that I could not make noise when he was asleep in the daytime. He was the lawgiver in our family and I never laughed in his presence" (16). Instead, the child "lurks timidly" around the kitchen doorway, *awed* by the figure of this "alien and remote" stranger whose mere presence compels him to repress his desire to make noise, to laugh, and perhaps, to *be* like him.

The incident with the kitten offers Richard a way to retaliate, to hit back at his father, not only for shouting at him, but for taking up so much space in the "orbit" of his concern. All he has to do is obey his father's command to kill the kitten that has been disturbing his sleep. Richard does just that, fully aware that his father's words were not meant to be taken literally. "I knew that he had not really meant for me to kill the kitten, but my deep hate of him urged me toward a literal acceptance of his word (17). With the deed done, Richard anticipates with pleasure the moment when he can subvert his father's authority by imitating his speech, by speaking his words: "Kill that damn thing!" (17). Richard knows that by punishing him, his father would be compromising his authority as the lawgiver in the family since his only disobedient act was to do exactly as he was told. Consequently, Richard emerges victorious against the man whose word was law: "I had had my first triumph over my father. I had made him believe that I had taken his words literally. He could not punish me now without risking his authority. I was happy because I had at last found a way to throw my criticism of him into his face. I had made him feel that, if he whipped me for killing the kitten, I would never give serious weight to his words again" (19).

Richard escapes physical punishment. His father does not exercise his paternal right and whip him. In that sense, he has effected a disruption or subversion within the symbolic order. But through the intervention of his mother, the order is reimposed. By waiting until dark and then demanding that he take the dead kitten down from its crude gallows and bury it, Richard's mother frightens him into submission before the Law of God the Father. Afterward, she leads him in a prayer for forgiveness:

> "Dear God, our Father, forgive me, for I knew not what I was doing. . . ."
> "Dear God, our Father, forgive me, for I knew not what I was doing," I repeated. (20)

Repentance can only come with contrition, and by the time his mother has completed her last phrase, "And while I sleep tonight, do not snatch the breath of life from me," Richard is so contrite, his mind so "frozen with horror," that he can only sob a terrified no. Alas, poor Richard! With the weight of the wrong he has committed upon him, he goes to bed hoping he'll never encounter a kitten again (20–21).

In *I Know Why the Caged Bird Sings,* Maya is similarly required by the mother to appeal to the father for forgiveness. Her "crime" has to do with saying what she did not mean, with her innocent articulation of the phrase "by the way." This simple construction which, as Bailey points out, is used by "whitefolks" (and most other folks) to mean "while we're on the subject," has a very different meaning for Momma Henderson. It is blasphemous. So after having offered to God the Father her redeeming prayer and having performed the redeeming function of whipping her granddaughter with a "long, ropy, peach-tree switch," she explains that since "Jesus was the Way, the Truth and the Light," to say "by the way" is to say "by Jesus," or "by God" (86). By saying "by the way," Marguerite, as she now called herself, had violated the Law of the Father: she had taken his name in vain. For this, the child must repent. And just as in *Black Boy,* it is the mother who leads Richard through the prayer; Maya's ritual of repentance is carried out by Momma Henderson. With Maya and Bailey kneeling by her side, she offers up a passionate prayer for forgiveness to the Father (86). In the final analysis, then, while the father may be the lawgiver, it is the mother who guarantees the authority of the law. In fact, in Lacanian terms, the law of the father takes on value only insofar as it is recognized by the mother as such.

It is also the mother who must protect the lawgiving phallus. For while Lacan defines the phallus as a "free-floating signifier" in the "psycho-analytic account of sexuality" (FS 74), in the social order within which Richard and Maya struggle to survive, the phallus becomes an organizing principle in a very real sense. The fear of castration likewise must be taken literally since, as the many documented accounts of lynching have demonstrated, the great *desire* of some folks within this order is to deprive black men of their penises. This fear is what holds in place the otherwise unstable racial categories of black and white. In both narratives, racial difference is defined in terms of the fearful power white people exercise over blacks.

Richard's curiosity about racial difference(s) is linked to his developing literacy. The more he reads, the more he learns of current events from the newspapers his mother teaches him to read, the more curious he becomes about events in his own neighborhood: "Everything happening in the neighborhood, no matter how trivial, became my business. It was in this manner that I first stumbled upon the relations between whites and blacks, and what I learned frightened me" (30). What he learned was that the right to beat a child was not just a *paternal* right. What he learned was that a "white" man could beat a "black" boy and not only not be his father; he didn't have to be any kin to him at all (31). In a gesture that anticipates by about fifty years Henry Louis Gates's explosive bracketing of the word race in the title of *"Race," Writing, and Difference,*[27] Wright places "black" and "white" in quotation marks in order to underscore the uselessness of these troublesome terms for understanding racial differences. For, to reiterate Gates's rhetorical question, "Who has seen a black or red person, a white, yellow, or brown?"[28] This is precisely the question Richard ponders as he tries to sort out for himself the implications of the report circulating in the neighborhood that a "white" man severely *beat*—not *whipped*—a "black" boy who was not his child:

> I had seen white men and women upon the streets a thousand times, but they had never looked particularly "white." To me they were merely people like other people, yet somehow strangely different because I had never come in close touch with any of them. For the most part I never thought of them; they simply existed somewhere in the background

of the city as a whole. It might have been that my tardiness in learning
to sense white people as "white" people came from the fact that many
of my relatives were "white"—looking people. My grandmother, who
was white as any "white" person, had never looked "white" to me. (31)

In what can be read as a kind of dialogue between the two texts, Wright
dramatizes, through Richard's persistent questions about Granny's whiteness, what Gates argues in *"Race," Writing, and Difference:* that "these
terms are arbitrary constructs, not reports of reality."[29] According to
Gates, they are nothing more than adjectives used as metaphors to differ-
entiate one group of people from another.[30] This becomes more apparent
to Richard as he and his mother, after having visited his grandmother
in Jackson, Mississippi, prepare to board a train for Arkansas where his
Aunt Maggie lives: "for the first time I noticed that there were two lines
of people at the ticket window, a 'white' line and a 'black' line. During my visit at Granny's a sense of the two races had been born in me
with a sharp concreteness that would never die until I died" (55). But
Richard's growing sense of the two races only complicates the problem
of where Granny and his other "white" looking relatives are placed along
the color line. For if that placement is determined by one's physical features, Granny is, in Richard's opinion, most certainly *mis*-placed. In an
attempt to understand these complex racial distinctions, Richard asks his
mother, "Is Granny white?"

> "If you've got eyes, you can see what color she is," my mother said.
> "I mean, do the white folks think she's white?"
> "Why don't you ask the white folks that?" she countered.
> "But you know," I insisted.
> "Why should I know?" she asked. "I'm not white."
> "Granny looks white," I said, hoping to establish one fact, at least.
> "Then why is she living with us colored folks?"
> "Don't you want Granny to live with us?" she asked, blunting my
> question.
> "Yes."
> "Then why are you asking?"
> "I want to *know.*"
> "Doesn't Granny live with us?"
> "Yes."
> "Isn't that enough?"
> "But does she *want* to live with us?"

"Why didn't you ask Granny that?" my mother evaded me again in a taunting voice.

"Did Granny become colored when she married Grandpa?"

"Will you stop asking silly questions!"

"But did she?"

"Granny didn't *become* colored," my mother said angrily. "She was *born* the color she is now." (56)

Needless to say, Richard's mother's responses do little to explain how Granny, despite her whiteness, ended up living with colored rather than white people. Instead, they provoke a certain uneasiness in Richard that she is holding something back, that something insidious lurks beneath the surface of her discourse, something she simply does not want him to know. What he does not understand is that like most "black" mothers of "black" sons, she knows that he will know soon enough. Hers is what Angelou in *I Know Why the Caged Bird Sings* describes as the plight of the Southern black woman. When it comes to her sons, grandsons, nephews, and lovers, for that matter, her heartstrings are tied to a hanging noose (95). Richard learns very soon, too soon, since his Uncle Hoskins is shot shortly after he and his mother arrive in Arkansas, that the fear of the hanging noose and of armed white men is as much a part of his cultural heritage as his instinctive mistrust of the Jews or the "traditional racial roles" he and the other black boys begin to play with the white boys "as though we *had been born to them,* as though it was in our blood, as though we were being guided by instinct" (93, emphasis added).

In *I Know Why the Caged Bird Sings,* Maya first experiences this fear when Stamps's "used-to-be" sheriff comes to warn Momma Henderson that Willie should lay low because "[a] crazy nigger messed with a white lady today," and that the "boys" will be coming by later (14). Momma Henderson acts quickly and instinctively. She knows only too well that when the "boys" go out riding in the name of white womanhood, somebody is bound to end up like the man Bailey claims had been shot in the head and thrown in a pond with his "things" cut off and put in his pocket "because the whitefolks said he did 'it' to a white woman" (30).

As soon as the "used-to-be" sheriff leaves, Momma Henderson and the children hide Willie in the bottom of the onion and potato bin. Maya recalls that "[i]t took him forever before he lay down flat, and then we covered him with potatoes and onions, layer upon layer, like a casserole. Grandmother knelt praying in the darkened store" (14–15).

For Maya *whitefolks* constitute the "alien other" long before they become part of her external reality. She derives her image of them from the
overheard utterances of the grownups who visit the store. However, the
image she constructs makes it impossible for her to conceive of them as
people. She finds it hard to believe that they are "really real." Not even
their underwear—proof positive that they possess genitalia like other
people—can convince her that whitefolks are real (20). They are too different and too dreadful to fit into the category "people" as she understands it: "People were those who lived on my side of town. I didn't like
them all, or, in fact, any of them very much, but they were people. These
others, the strange pale creatures that lived in their alien unlife, weren't
considered folks. They were whitefolks" (21, emphasis added). Whenever
some of these *others*—the "powhitetrash children" who lived on Momma
Henderson's land—invaded the store, Maya claims that she would pinch
one of them, not only because of her anger and frustration over the liberties they took, but also because she didn't believe in their "flesh reality"
(22). Yet the image of whitefolks is one of two images that perform the
essential function, in writing, of *in-forming,* or giving form to, Maya as a
racial and gender-specific subject.[31] The other is the image of the symbolic
phallus, which, as I will discuss later, is represented by her relationships
with her brother, Bailey, and the man who rapes her, Mr. Freeman. What
I would like to take up now is how what Lacan calls the "image" helps to
structure the psychological reality of the subject, or the *I,* in Angelou's
and Wright's "auto-texts."

In his seminal essay on the function of the *I* in psychoanalytic experience,[32] Lacan distinguishes two forms of *I:* the "Ideal" or specular *I,* and
the social *I.* At various stages of the child's psychic and social maturation, each *I* plays an important role in identity formation. The "Ideal-I"
is predicated upon the unified specular image that the child in the mirror
stage recognizes as its own.[33] It is the form the *I* takes before its objectification in the "dialectic of identification with the other, and before
language restores to it, in the universal, its function as subject" (*Ecrits* 2).
For Lacan, the "Ideal-I" is the primary source of identification. By identifying with this *I,* the child assumes an image of itself as a complete and
unified being. The "Ideal-I" is also seen as the source of the secondary
identifications that will situate the "agency of the ego, before its social
determination, in a fictional direction" (*Ecrits* 2).

John Muller and William Richardson write, in *Lacan and Language,*
that Lacan's use of the term "fictional" can be understood in two ways.

The first has to do with the "fictional quality" of the "primitive alien-ation" the subject experiences as it is "fixed," by the model of the "Ideal-I," into an ideal of a total unity that is unattainable (31). The second has to do with the fact that the mirror reflects an inverted image of what stands before it. What the child initially experiences, then, is an inverted image of the "external world with all its spatial relationships." The relationship that the mirror-image presumably establishes between the "organism and its reality" is therefore distorted. This "primitive distortion" is what ac-counts for the fictional quality of the "ego's experience of reality" and its subsequent confusions and misidentifications:

> Given the fact that the infant subject first discovers himself in an ex-ternal image, it is easy to understand how he confuses this external image of himself with the images of other subjects among whom he finds himself. It is in such fashion that the "social dialectic" begins. This confusion leads to a misidentification of himself with the other and has far-reaching effects, not only on relationships with others but on knowledge of external things as well. This new development, called "transitivism" by Lacan, is the result of "a veritable captation by the image of the other." (*Lacan and Language*, 30–31)

This new development marks the deflection of the specular *I* into the social *I*. It marks the point in the child's maturation when everything, all knowledge, is culturally mediated through the desire of the other (*Ecrits* 5–6).

In "Du Boisian" terms, Maya's misidentification of herself with her socially constructed other, which results in the failure of her memory at the crucial moment when she is to recite a poem during her church's Easter Sunday service, can be read as an instance of double-consciousness at work in the text. Painfully conscious of her lavender taffeta dress and her skinny legs, which she believes to be the focus of everyone's atten-tion, Maya cannot get beyond the first two lines of the poem: "What you looking at me for?/I didn't come to stay" (1). Maya had watched Momma Henderson alter the dress she was to wear on Easter Sunday and had imagined that the finished product would somehow magically trans-form her into the image of "one of the sweet little white girls who were everybody's dream of what was right with the world" (1). Like magic, Marguerite would be mistaken for someone else. People would run up to her and say, "Marguerite [sometimes it was 'dear Marguerite'], forgive us, please, we didn't know who you were." And Marguerite would answer generously, "No, you couldn't have known. Of course I forgive you" (1–2). But, alas, poor Maya! By Easter morning the dress has lost its appeal. Not even Momma Henderson's excellent dressmaking skills could conceal the fact that Maya's Easter outfit was "a plain ugly cut-down from a white woman's once-was-purple throwaway" which, despite its "old-lady-long," did not hide her skinny greased and dust-covered legs.

Maya's forgetfulness on Easter Sunday occurs by dint of repression: "I hadn't so much forgot as I couldn't bring myself to remember. Other things were more important" (1). Like the autobiographer, Maya "forgets" the unimportant things—the next two lines of her poem—in order to tell us something about the self. The reiterated lines express a truth: "What you looking at me for? / I didn't come to stay." Maya *does not* stay. After having been prompted by the minister's wife to utter the last two lines of the poem, Maya leaves, but not before desecrating the church with her urine. As she runs from the church, Maya's fluids swell up despite the pressure she exerts to hold them back. Turbulent, excessive, they seep through her orifice until she finally lets them go. The "sweet release"—the *jouissance*—Maya experiences when her fluids finally overflow the boundaries of her yet undeveloped body gives way to the greater joy of knowing that not only had she liberated herself, at least for the moment, from the "silly church"; she had done so without dying of the busted head she was sure she would get from running and crying and trying so hard not to pee (3).

During a subsequent Sunday church service Maya does not even try to control herself. The service had become such a spectacle that Maya simply could not contain her laughter or her urine despite Momma Henderson's threatening glares. Sister Monroe is the person responsible for turning the orderly service into chaos. Unable to attend church regularly, she makes up for her absences with an excess of shouts of praise to the Lord and screams to the Reverend to "Preach it" (32).

Maya and Bailey first witness Sister Monroe's formidable Holy Spirit–inspired "happiness" when she returns to church after a particularly long absence—she had taken a few months off to have a baby. On that day, the spirit hit her so hard that none of the ushers or deacons could hold her down or keep her from the pulpit where the Reverend continued preaching despite the pandemonium spreading around him. The more the Reverend preached, the louder Sister Monroe screamed "preach it" and the harder she tried to grab hold of him. The intense call and response pattern that is established between the screaming woman and the preaching man

causes Sister Willson and Deacon Jackson to come under the influence of
the powerful spirit of the Holy Ghost. Like Sister Monroe, they make the
Reverend the recipient of all of their pent-up agressions. Deacon Jackson
punches Reverend Taylor and gets punched back. Sister Willson pulls his
tie. And to the astonishment of the congregation, the three of them end
up on the floor while Sister Monroe, "cool and spent," steps off the dias
and reinstitutes order by leading the congregation in a hymn about how
she *came* to Jesus and He made her glad (32–33, emphasis added).

Sister Monroe repeats her Sunday morning performance with Reverend Thomas, the greedy chicken eating preacher who Maya and Bailey
both despise. While she was too astonished to laugh before, the spectacle of Sister Monroe chasing Reverend Thomas around the church and
screaming "I say, preach it" and beating him on the head with her purse
until his false teeth jump out is too much for Maya. This time nothing,
not even Momma Henderson's stern warning can keep Maya from laugh-
ing and peeing as she and Bailey slide off their bench and onto the floor:

> There was more laughter in me trying to get out. I didn't know there
> was that much in the whole world. It pressed at all my body openings,
> forcing everything in its path. I cried and hollered, passed gas and
> urine. I didn't see Bailey descend to the floor, but I rolled over once
> and he was kicking and screaming too. Each time we looked at each
> other we howled louder than before, and though he tried to say some-
> thing, the laughter attacked him and he was only able to get out "I
> say, preach." And then I rolled over onto Uncle Willie's rubber-tipped
> cane. (36–37)

Once again, Maya violates the rules prescribing proper behavior in the
church. Once again, Maya subordinates her fear of the inevitable whipping to the sweet release brought on, this time, by the return of the re-
pressed. Once again, Maya's memory fails her: she has no memory of how
she and Bailey got from the church to the parsonage. What she remem-
bers is that the whipping was almost as disruptive to the Sunday service
as Sister Moore's *jouissance*. While they are receiving the "whipping of
[their] lives," Bailey adopts a "scream as loud as possible so the whipper
will become embarrassed" strategy that causes the minister's wife to ask
Uncle Willie to quiet the children down so that the service can continue
(37). Order is once again restored in the church. But for weeks afterward,
all Bailey has to do is say "preach it" to make his sister laugh until she
cried (37).

Before the St. Louis rape episode, Maya's relationship with Bailey is privileged in every way. With her mother and "symbiotic All" absent and presumed dead (Maya can only picture her mother as lying in a coffin with her black hair "spread out on a tiny white pillow"), Maya mediates her need for wholeness through the image of her "pretty Black brother:" "Of all the needs (there are none imaginary) a lonely child has, the one that must be satisfied, if there is going to be hope and a hope of wholeness, is the unshaking need for an unshakable God. My pretty Black brother was my Kingdom Come" (19).

Maya's image of Bailey is an important element in the complex or "constellation of images" with which she (mis)identifies.[34] Like the mother, Bailey represents everything Maya is not but "wants-to-be." He is "small, graceful and smooth" with "velvet-black skin" and curly black hair. She is "big, elbowy and grating" with a head "covered with black steel wool" (17). What causes Maya to elevate Bailey to the status of an unshakable God is his refusal to place a negative value on her physical appearance. He fulfills, at least for a while, her desire for recognition by the Other. But alas, poor Maya! Even unshakable Gods, and especially eight-year-old ones, sometimes fail. When, through the intervention of their father, the children are reunited with their mother, Bailey forgets how he and his sister shared the pain of being "unwanted" and falls "instantly and forever in love" (50).

Angelou's contextualization of this moment is crucial for our understanding of how Maya comes to (mis)identify with Mr. Freeman as yet another substitute for the mother. She stages the event in such a way that Maya is clearly marginalized by Bailey's desire for the forbidden and often inaccessible mother: "She was *his* Mother Dear and I resigned myself to his condition. They were more alike than she and I, or even he and I. They both had physical beauty and personality, so I figured it figured" (50, emphasis added).

Bailey's (Oedipal) condition, his "mother-(re)attachment" marks what Juilette Mitchell, following Freud, would call his entrance into his phallic heritage—"She was *his* Mother Dear—," and Maya's symbolic castration or detachment from the object of her unrequited love. The "path to 'normal' womanhood" requires that since the female child lacks the law-giving phallus and "can no more physiologically possess her mother than culturally she must ever be allowed to wish to do so," she must shift her desire from the mother to the father.[35] The problem for Maya is that her father is as illusory as the always absent mother.

Bailey Senior abruptly appeared in Stamps one morning and shattered the elaborate fantasies she had constructed of him. The (un)reality of his existence exceeded her imaginary inventions and caused her to wonder if this was, in fact, her real father. To complicate matters, Bailey Senior promised to take the children to California, but he takes them to St. Louis instead. This change in their itinerary further distances Maya from the man who claimed to be her father. St. Louis, with its "new kind of hot" and "new kind of dirty," is so alien to anything pictured in her memory that Maya wonders if he isn't really the devil delivering his children to Hell (49). Furthermore, Bailey Senior does not remain in St. Louis long enough for his "baby girl" to shift her mother-love onto him. He delivers the children to their mother at Grandmother Baxter's house, then leaves for California a few days later, no less a stranger than when he had abruptly arrived in Stamps, Arkansas.

With her father out of the way, Maya only has Bailey to compete with for her mother's love during the six months they remain in Grandmother Baxter's house. During that time, the children rarely see their mother in the house. She has them meet her instead at Louie's Tavern where a kind of Freudian *fort-da*[36] game is acted out between the dancing mother and the desiring daughter: "Mother would dance alone in front of us to music from the Seeburg. I loved her most at those times. She was like a pretty kite that floated just above my head. If I liked, I could pull it in to me by saying I had to go to the toilet or by starting a fight with Bailey. I never did either, but the *power* made me tender to her" (55, emphasis added). Like the child who in the Freudian model learns to master the absence of the loved and needed object through its symbolic *fort-da* play,[37] Maya attempts to master her anxiety over her mother's comings and goings by securing for herself, through her metaphor of the pretty kite which she can pull into herself at will, the power promised by the symbolic phallus. The problem is that, unlike her brother who enters fully into his phallic heritage, Maya suppresses her power, however illusory it may be. The unspoken threat of being sent away is greater than her desire to *be-as-one* with the mother whose realness she is never able to "put [her] finger on" in the first place (57). With the burden of this threat bearing heavily upon her, Maya turns to the only person with whom she can identify—her mother's boyfriend, Mr. Freeman.

While it is not my intention to romanticize the rape of Maya Angelou or deflect the guilt from the substitute father/mother onto the violated child, I think it is worth noting how Angelou's contextualization of

Maya's relationship to Mr. Freeman in some ways underscores the insta-
bility of masculine/feminine gender arrangements. Mr. Freeman's *crime*
most certainly places him in the masculine register. But with breasts that
"lay on his chest like flat titties" he also figures as a kind of maternal metaphor. Furthermore, in what amounts to a reversal of gender roles, it is
Mr. Freeman who brings in the necessities and stays with the children in
the evenings while their mother, who was trained as a nurse, cuts poker
games in gambling parlors in order to earn extra money (58). In other
words, the mother is made present in her absence(s) through the image
of Mr. Freeman whose primary preoccupation is to passively wait for her
to return:

> Mr. Freeman moved gracefully, like a big brown bear, and seldom
> spoke to us. He simply waited for Mother and put his whole self into
> the waiting. He never read the paper or patted his foot to radio. He
> waited. That was all.
>
> If she came home before we went to bed, we saw the man come
> alive. He would start out of the big chair, like a man coming out of
> sleep, smiling. (59)

Or like the child in the *fort-da* game whose "o-o-o-o" expresses its satisfaction with the return of the desired mother-object.[38] The mother rewards
his waiting by sitting on his lap, an act that Maya later mimes when, in
another reversal of roles, she begins to wait for him.

Maya's waiting marks an important point on what Juliette Mitchell,
following Freud, blithely calls the "path to 'normal' womanhood." It
marks the point at which the child, with great pain and confusion,
effectively shifts her mother-attachment to a desire for recognition by
the man she (mis)identifies as her real father. Needless to say, Maya's
(mis)indentification occurs under anything but normal circumstances,
although for the child, sleeping in the big bed with her mother and her
mother's lover is nothing out of the ordinary. Maya had always slept
with Momma Henderson and found nothing strange about sleeping in
her mother's big bed, particularly since this arrangement was intended
to help her overcome her "horrifying nightmares." What Maya does find
strange is the pressure she feels from the soft, "mushy and squirmy," but
unnamed "thing" resting on her leg when she wakes up one morning and
finds that her mother, who had an errand to run, had left her alone in the
bed with Mr. Freeman.

After assuring her that he is not going to hurt her, Mr. Freeman draws the unafraid but somewhat apprehensive child onto his chest and into a labyrinth of contradictory wishes and desires. As Mr. Freeman masturbates, Maya goes from fearing that his accelerated heartbeat will cause him to die while holding her to feeling a sense of being at home with her real father when it is all over: "Finally he was quiet, and then came the nice part. He held me so softly that I wished he wouldn't ever let me go. I felt at home. From the way he was holding me I knew he'd never let me go or let anything bad ever happen to me. This was probably my real father and we had found each other at last. But then he rolled over, leaving me in a wet place and stood up" (61). Maya's illusion of wholeness is abruptly shattered when Mr. Freeman, in order to cover up his crime, accuses her of having peed in the bed. To further complicate matters, Mr. Freeman demands absolute silence about what "they" have done although it is not clear to Maya just what it is that "they" have done. Mr. Freeman warns Maya that if she tells anyone, he will kill her brother Bailey.

And so, with this new burden of guilt loaded upon the already existing burden of the threat of being sent away from the beloved mother, Maya is thrust onto a not-so-normal "path" to womanhood. Sworn to silence, she must sort out, all by herself, the "quandary" within which she finds herself: "It was the same old quandary. I had always lived it. There was an army of adults, whose motives and movements I just couldn't understand and who made no effort to understand mine. There was never any question of my disliking Mr. Freeman, I simply didn't understand him either" (62). But in the absence of the real father, Mr. Freeman is the only person onto whom she can effectively *displace* her mother-love. With her brother's abdication from his "God-like" position and her mother's inaccessibility, Mr. Freeman becomes the new center of her world and the (crooked) conduit for her painful passage from childhood to 'normal' womanhood, a passage that traverses the course of the two seduction scenes leading up to the rape episode.

In the weeks following her first seduction, Maya begins to miss "the encasement of [Mr. Freeman's] big arms" and the satisfaction she derived from her first physical contact with someone who existed outside of her childhood realm of "Bailey, food, Momma, the Store, reading books and Uncle Willie" (62). But Mr. Freeman refuses to acknowledge her presence until, one evening, she willfully sits on his lap:

> One evening, when I couldn't concentrate on anything, I went over to him and sat quickly on his lap. He had been waiting for Mother

again. Bailey was listening to *The Shadow* and didn't miss me. At first Mr. Freeman sat still, not holding me or anything, then I felt a soft lump under my thigh begin to move. It twitched against me and started to harden. Then he pulled me to his chest. He smelled of coal dust and grease and he was so close I buried my face in his shirt and listened to his heart, it was beating just for me. (63)

This illusion of being at one with the disliked but desired object is once again ruptured when Mr. Freeman suddenly stands up and runs to the bathroom. For months afterward he refuses to speak to her. Hurt and confused, Maya retreats into the fictional universe of Horatio Alger whose "heroes were always good, always won, and were always boys." Tiny Tim becomes a hero with whom she can identify, and the Katzenjammer kids amuse her because they always "made the adults look stupid" (63–64). The boys' heroism crowds her imagination until she forgets about Mr. Freeman and how he held her "precious." But one morning, after the mother fails to come home from one of her evening outings, Mr. Freeman brutally forces his way into Maya's newly constructed world of fiction and the imagination and into her "eight-year-old body," thereby definitively changing the course of her path to "normal" womanhood.

In an attempt to cover up his crime, Mr. Freeman bathes the badly abused child and then sends her to the library where she has difficulty sitting on the hard seats because "they had been constructed for children" (66). This implies that Maya already feels that she no longer fits into the category "children" although she invokes a child's rhyme as she tries, with great pain, to make her way back to her mother's house: "Thrum . . . step . . . thrum . . . step . . . STEP ON THE CRACK . . . thrum . . . step" (66). But that's not all there is to the rhyme. A more complete version would go like this: Thrum . . . step . . . thrum . . . step . . . STEP ON THE CRACK . . . Thrum . . . step . . . thrum . . . step . . . *BREAK YOUR MOTHER'S BACK*. Maya leaves the last line out. This makes me wonder if Maya, by dint of omission, is not silently expressing her rage that her mother did not come home in time to prevent the rape. Or, perhaps this is her way of exonerating her mother from any blame for Mr. Freeman's crime. For let us not forget, Maya idealizes her mother and attributes a great deal of power to her. "She was educated, from a well-known family, and after all, wasn't she born in St. Louis" (58)? She was also a good provider, "even if that meant getting someone else to furnish the provisions" (58).

In a sense, Maya becomes both the provider and the provisions as

Mr. Freeman takes advantage of her mother's absences and abuses her sexually. However, I would not go so far as to place the blame for the child's rape on the mother as Mary Jane Lupton does in "Singing the Black Mother: Maya Angelou and Autobiographical Continuity." Reiterating Maya's earlier impression that her mother was "too beautiful to have children," Lupton writes, "Ironically, this mother 'too beautiful to have children' is to a large degree responsible for her own child's brutal rape." She cites an essay by Stephanie Demetrakopoulos, "The Metaphysics of Matrilinearism in Women's Autobiography"[39] to support her argument that Mr. Freeman, who is constantly waiting for Vivian to return, " 'uses Angelou as an extension of her mother' to satisfy his sexual urges." Lupton adds that "It could also be suggested that Vivian uses Maya, somehow knowing that in her own absence Maya will keep her lover amused."[40]

These interpretations are consistent with what Janet Liebman Jacobs in "Reassessing Mother Blame in Incest" calls the "mother as colluder" theory of incestuous relationships; that is, the mother, by withdrawing from her sexual role, sets the daughter up in an incestuous relationship with the father or father/substitute.[41] Needless to say, Maya's mother does indeed "set her up" when she "withdraws" from the big bed and leaves her alone with Mr. Freeman. But Maya's rape is *Mr. Freeman's* crime and not the mother's. Furthermore, what Demetrakopoulos and Lupton overlook is that Angelou structures the rape scene around a fantasy. As Maya confronts her evil perpetrator, she expects that at any moment her "mother or Bailey or the Green Hornet" will "bust down the door and save" her (65). This illusion of maternal power and protectiveness would most certainly have been shattered as Mr. Freeman broke into and entered Maya's "eight-year-old body" and then dared her not to tell. Like the incest victims described in Jacobs's "Reassessing Mother Blame in Incest," Maya experiences the real "powerlessness of women in the most personal and painful of ways, first through her own victimization and then through the knowledge of her mother's ineffectuality." It should be noted that Jacobs does not attribute this "ineffectuality" to any kind of dysfunction on the part of the mother, but rather to the "real power relations of paternal control and dominance."[42]

Maya's mother is rendered ineffectual by what she has not been told. When she returns home to find Maya sick and in bed, she begins to treat her for measles since it was said to be "going around the neighborhood" and since Maya doesn't tell her anything different (67). Ignoring

Mr. Freeman's argument that Bailey should not be allowed in the room with Maya "unless you want a house full of sick children," Vivian Baxter orders Bailey to come with her and get cool towels to wipe his sister's feverish face. As soon as they leave the room, Mr. Freeman approaches the bed and again prohibits her from speaking by threatening to kill Bailey. "He leaned over, his whole face a threat that could have smothered me. 'If you tell . . .' And again so softly, I almost didn't hear it—'If you tell'" (67). In this way, Mr. Freeman controls the situation and seriously undermines Maya's image of her mother as the most powerful figure in her emotional life.[43] Moreover, when Maya wakes up during the night and hears her mother and Mr. Freeman arguing, she finally realizes that Vivian Baxter is as vulnerable to Mr. Freeman's violence as she is. "I couldn't hear what they were saying, but I did hope that she wouldn't make him so mad that he'd hurt her too. I knew he could do it, with his cold face and empty eyes" (67).

Maya finds little consolation in her mother's announcement the next day that Mr. Freeman has moved out. Confused about her own role in the assault and afraid for her brother Bailey, Maya longs for death so long as she can die away from Mr. Freeman, who she believes has control even over her death. "I knew I was dying and, in fact, I longed for death, but I didn't want to die anywhere near Mr. Freeman. I knew that even now he wouldn't have allowed death to have me unless he wished it to" (68). Maya therefore continues to silently endure her pain and humiliation until her soiled underwear fall at her mother's feet while Bailey is changing her linen. With the evidence out in the open, Maya still refuses to tell her mother what happened. Bailey gets her to tell "who did that" to her by convincing her that he won't let the man kill him (69). Bailey in turn gives the information to Grandmother Baxter who has Mr. Freeman arrested, thereby sparing him, at least for the duration of his trial, "the awful wrath of [Maya's] pistol-whipping uncles" (69).

Maya's own rage finds its proper object during the trial when Mr. Freeman's lawyer asks her whether "the accused" had tried to touch her prior to the time she *said* he raped her. Maya knows instinctively that the people packed into the courtroom expect her to say no. In order to avoid lying, she therefore retreats into silence only to be summoned back into speech by the lawyer's question: "Did the accused touch you before the occasion on which you claim he raped you?" (71). Knowing that the answer is yes but that she must say no, Maya screams her rage at Mr. Freeman, not for having raped her, but for making her tell a lie. "How I despised the man for making me lie. Old, mean, nasty thing. Old, black, nasty thing. The tears didn't soothe my heart as they usually did. I screamed, 'Ole, mean, dirty thing, you. Dirty old thing.' Our lawyer brought me off the stand and to my mother's arms. The fact that I had arrived at my *desired* destination by lies made it less appealing to me" (71, emphasis added).

Françoise Lionnet explains in *Autobiographical Voices* that it is during the trial that Maya begins to internalize the religious teachings of her childhood and to perceive herself as an evil person.[44] Her guilt and negative self-perception are intensified when she learns that Mr. Freeman, who was released from custody after the trial, has been murdered. Forgetting the crime he committed against her, Maya mistakenly attributes his death to her lie and decides that a man's life is too high a price to pay for "one lie" (72). Taking her cue from Grandmother Baxter, who forbids the children from ever mentioning "that evil man's name" in her house again, Maya decides that the only way to keep the "evilness" in her body from rushing off her tongue and escaping and flooding "the world and all the innocent people" is to stop talking to everyone except her brother Bailey (72–73). As Lionnet puts it, when Maya discovers that language as "powerful performance" can kill, she "metaphorically cuts off her own tongue."[45] However, her contention that Maya "removes herself from the community by refusing language" suggests that Lionnet has not sufficiently reflected on the relationship between language and human beings.[46] As I have tried to argue in my chapter on Senghor and Césaire, language is that which establishes a community between beings and the world. Or, lest we forget, let me cite Heidegger's *On the Way to Language* once again: "In order to be who we are, we human beings remain committed to and within the being of language, and can never step out of it and look at it from somewhere else."[47] Maya, therefore, *cannot* refuse language. The essence of her being as human being remains irrevocably entangled in the "mesh of relations" that constitute language as such.[48] Maya does refuse to *speak*, however. In so doing, she achieves a "perfect personal silence" that allows her to be-in-the-world in a much more primordial way:

> I discovered that to achieve perfect personal silence all I had to do was to attach myself leechlike to sound. I began to listen to everything. I probably hoped that after I had heard all the sounds, really heard them and packed them down, deep in my ears, the world would be quiet around me. I walked into rooms where people were laughing,

their voices hitting the walls like stones, and I simply stood still—in the midst of the riot of sound. After a minute or two, silence would rush into the room from its hiding place because I had eaten up all the sounds. (73)

This kind of hearing transcends what for Heidegger is the psychological definition of hearing as the "sensing of tones and the perception of sounds."[49] Maya "eats up" the sounds that provide phenomenal evidence of the material world. By packing those sounds down deep into her ears, she begins to clear the way for a more authentic kind of hearing and understanding. The ensuing silence is a necessary condition for achieving what Heidegger calls "the appropriating, initiating movement within the being of language."[50]

In other words, Maya's silence allows her to speak more profoundly about the "peculiar property of language," that is, language's exclusive concern with itself.[51] When she and Bailey return to Stamps, for example, Maya *listens* as Bailey who, by imitating his father "speaking the King's English with a big city accent," carefully crafts fictions about their experiences up North for the people who visit Momma Henderson's store (75). Her concern is with how he weaves a "tapestry of entertainment for them" that "was as foreign to him as it was to [her]" (75), and how his "double entendres" and "two-pronged sentences" escape the comprehension of the people who are the targets of his sarcasm. Everything else pales against her "silver-tongued" brother who sounds "just like his daddy" (76). For nearly a year all other sounds come to Maya "dully, as if people were speaking through their handkerchiefs or with their hands over their mouths." Colors are perceived as "faded familiarities," while familiar names escape her memory to the point that she begins to worry about her sanity. "After all, we had been away less than a year, and customers whose accounts I had formerly remembered without consulting the ledger were now complete strangers" (77).

According to Lionnet, Angelou's self-imposed silence actually lasted much longer than a year. Lionnet cites a 1986 televised interview in which Angelou said, "From the age of seven-and-a-half till twelve, my whole body became one big ear: I *memorized poetry* but didn't speak . . . because my voice had killed that man."[52] Needless to say, Angelou is speaking metaphorically—her voice/Maya's voice did not kill that man. For let us not forget, Maya speaks during the trial in order to say *nothing* about the truth of her relationship with Mr. Freeman. Her refusal to speak after-

ward is an attempt to gain absolute control over what the critic Maurice
Blanchot, who also speaks metaphorically about the relation between the
voice—between speaking—and death, has called the power of speech to
annihilate—to kill—the very being of the thing being spoken about. In
"Literature and the Right to Death" Blanchot writes, "When I speak, I
deny the existence of what I am saying, but I also deny the existence of
the person who is saying it: if my speech reveals being in its nonexistence,
it also affirms that this revelation is made on the basis of the nonexistence
of the person making it, out of his power to remove himself from himself,
to be *other* than his being. This is why, if true language is to begin, the life
that will carry this language must have experienced its nothingness."[53] By
refusing to speak, by privileging the memory over the voice and by turning herself into one big ear, or as Derrida would put it, a "high-fidelity
receiver,"[54] Angelou opened up the possibility for "true language"—the
language of literature—to begin. Angelou's voice gives way to this nothingness in much the same way that Maya's silence, under the tutelage of
Mrs. Bertha Flowers, gives way to reading literature in a much more authentic way.

In *Autobiographical Voices*, Françoise Lionnet describes Maya's relationship with Mrs. Flowers as one based on that bankrupt sociological concept of the *role model*. "She is a maternal and nurturing figure like Momma,
but her aristocratic demeanor and formal education make her an in-
stant role model for Maya, the imaginative reader of English novels."[55]
What Lionnet overlooks is that Maya does not initially experience Mrs.
Flowers as maternal or nurturing. Maya does not recognize those quali-
ties in Mrs. Flowers until years later when she realizes that except for her
formal education, Mrs. Flowers is much like Momma Henderson (78).
With her "printed voile dresses and flowered hats," and "rich black skin,"
Mrs. Flowers represents for Maya "the measure of what a human being
can be" (78). Ironically, however, Maya measures her against the fictional
feminine characters she encounters in her imaginative readings of English
novels:

> She appealed to me personally because she was like people I had never
> met personally. Like women in English novels who walked the moors
> (whatever they were) with their loyal dogs racing at a respectful dis-
> tance. Like the women who sat in front of roaring fireplaces, drinking
> tea incessantly from silver trays full of scones and crumpets. Women
> who walked over the "heath" and read morocco-bound books and had

two last names divided by a hyphen. It would be safe to say that she made me proud to be Negro, just by being her*self*. (79)

But that self is constituted, at least in Maya's imagination, as a highly idealized, and one might add phallogocentric, image of the feminine Other. For as Sandra Gilbert and Susan Guber have shown in *The Mad-woman in the Attic,* the prototypical woman in the nineteenth-century English novel inhabits a claustrophobic fictional universe where she does little more than sit in front of roaring fireplaces, drinking tea incessantly, and suffering from boredom and intellectual loneliness and the "blazing fires" themselves.[56] One cannot help but wonder if what remains unwritten in Angelou's text about the women in English novels also informs on Mrs. Flowers's unwritten story. One cannot help but wonder if she, too, leads what Gilbert and Gubar have called "a posthumous existence in her own lifetime," a life that has no story beyond that of her own self-lessness.[57]

For Maya, Mrs. Flowers is a kind of *objet d'art*—not something to be emulated, as the concept of the role model implies,[58] but a "beautiful angel-woman" enshrined in a little bungalow up on the hill, beyond the "triangular farm on [the] left," and off the road leading down to Momma Henderson's store. Like Gilbert and Gubar's "angel-woman," Mrs. Flowers is, for the most part, alienated from the rest of the community and from "ordinary fleshly life."[59] It does not occur to Maya until she enters the house and smells the cookies Mrs. Flowers baked for her that her "angel-woman" would be involved with such "common experiences" as food and eating and defecating. "There must have been an outhouse, too, but my mind never recorded it" (82). What her mind does record is a room where "browned photographs leered or threatened from the walls and the white, freshly done curtains pushed against themselves and *against the wind*" as if to prevent fresh air from entering (83, emphasis added). Mrs. Flowers's story is undoubtedly inscribed and enframed in the photographs. But Maya, whose great concern is with preserving her image of Mrs. Flowers as a gentlewoman who transcends narrow racial categories, makes no attempt to read or interpret them. Indeed, when Mrs. Flowers returns from the kitchen with a platter of cookies covered with a tea towel, all that is needed to complete the claustrophobic scenario of the Victorian woman at home is a fireplace roaring with a blazing fire.

Maya's visit to Mrs. Flowers's house marks the first of her "lessons in living." While Maya nibbles "lady-like" on the cookies, Mrs. Flowers teaches her to value the "collective wisdom of generations" of "country people." Afterward, she brushes the cookie crumbs from the table and begins to read the opening passage of *A Tale of Two Cities*.

Angelou's description of Maya's reaction to the musical quality of Mrs. Flowers's voice is perhaps the most sensuous passage in the text. Maya *listens* with almost all of her senses as Mrs. Flowers reads, "It was the best of times and the worst of times. . . . Her voice slid in and curved down through and over the words. She was nearly singing. I wanted to look at the pages. Were they the same that I had read? Or were there notes, music, lined on the pages as in a hymn book? Her sounds began cascading gently. I knew from listening to a thousand preachers that she was nearing the end of her reading and I hadn't really heard, heard to understand, a single word" (84). Maya receives Mrs. Flowers's reading as a pure sensuous experience. The sounds emitted by Mrs. Flowers's voice cascade gently downward, deep into Maya's ears, through the auditory canal, and deeper, deeper into the labyrinth until they gently rest on the cochlea.

With the wonder of Mrs. Flowers's reading filling her ears and the "sweet vanilla flavor" from the cookies lingering on her tongue, Maya is seduced back into speech. Maya speaks. She utters a simple "Yes, ma'am" in appreciation for Mrs. Flowers's eloquent performance and is, in a sense, reborn. Mrs. Flowers is therefore a maternal metaphor only to the extent that she links Maya to her and to the *mother-tongue* — the King's English — through the ear or what Derrida, speaking metaphorically, refers to as the *omphalos,* which he describes as resembling "both an ear and a mouth" (and, I might add, a womb). "It has the invaginated folds and the involuted orificiality of both. Its center preserves itself at the bottom of an invisible, restless cavity that is sensitive to all waves which, whether or not they come from the outside, whether they are emitted or received, are always transmitted by this trajectory of obscure circumvolutions."[60]

Mrs. Flowers emits what she has received: the text of a "dead father" from a tradition littered with the remains of "dead fathers." Maya, "with an ear attuned to the name of the dead man and the living feminine" inherits this tradition and a sense of selflessness that allows her to hear herself speak her simple "Yes, ma'am."[61] As she races down the hill to share her experience and her cookies with Bailey, Maya tells herself that whatever prompted Mrs. Flowers to speak to her in the first place is irrevelant. "All I cared about was that she had made tea cookies for *me* and read to *me* from her favorite book. It was enough to prove that she liked me" (85).

But that *me* is both black and female. This raises the question of how to assert oneself as such in a socially constructed system that often refuses to even recognize your (proper) name. Maya learns from Bailey that sometimes it is necessary to find ways of disrupting the system. For example, when Mrs. Viola Cullinan refuses, for the sake of convenience, to call her by her name, Bailey instructs Maya to retaliate by breaking her favorite dishes.

The tactic works. Maya waits until she hears Mrs. Cullinan scream her (mis)name, then deliberately drops the serving tray containing the fish-shaped casserole and cups that once belonged to Mrs. Cullinan's mother. Hysterically, Mrs. Cullinan throws a piece of the broken glass at Maya but hits the cook Miss Glory "right over the ear" as she screams to her guests that her young maid's name is not Mary, but Margaret, although at that time Maya referred to herself as Marguerite (93). Mrs. Cullinan's ear is finally made keen enough, through the clatter of her momma's Virginia china hitting the kitchen floor, to hear Maya's name. Her voice completes what Derrida would call a contractural arrangement that allows the "autos" of Maya's autobiography to take place by reproducing her signature, her name. "Her name's Margaret, goddamn it, her name's Margaret" (93). In this way, it is the "ear of the other that signs." [62] Satisfied that she has been able to at least partially reconstitute herself as other than what Mrs. Cullinan initially perceived her to be, Maya walks out and leaves "the front door wide open so all the neighbors could hear" (93).

All that remains to be decided is how Maya is marked in terms of gender relations. We must not forget that the category *woman* was destabilized for Maya by the sporting men and women who flocked to the courtroom to hear the evidence of how she was sexually abused. The general consensus of the pin-stripe-suited gamblers and their "make-up deep" women who attended the trial was that now she knew as much as they did (70). Now she was no longer a child. Even the nurses in the hospital saw her rape as a kind of brutal rite of passage or initiation into womanhood. Consequently, Maya separates herself from the other children but knows better than to join the women.

The annual church picnic episode underscores Maya's dilemma. She refuses to participate in the children's games because she feels that she has outgrown them. Neither does she make herself useful as Momma

Henderson suggests. Instead, she stands around pondering the appropriate direction to take when the time comes for her to relieve herself.

> Signs with arrows around the barbecue pit pointed MEN, WOMEN, CHILDREN, toward fading lanes, grown over since last year. Feeling ages old and very wise at ten, I couldn't allow myself to be found by small children squatting behind a tree. Neither did I have the nerve to follow the arrow pointing the way for WOMEN. If any grownup had caught me there, it was possible that she'd think I was being *"woman-ish"* and would report me to Momma, and I knew what I could expect from her. So when the urge hit me to relieve myself, I headed toward another direction. Once through the wall of sycamore trees *I found myself* in a clearing ten times smaller than the picnic area and cool and quiet. (117, emphasis added)

Maya finds a space for herself in the clearing. Here the world with its categories and delineations is temporarily suspended. It comes to her only as sound ("the children's voices") and smell ("the thick odor of food cooking over open fires") as she leans against the roots of a tree and experiences the strange sensation of falling upward into a blue cloud in the "uneven circle of the sky" (117). Maya feels as if the natural order of the universe has suddenly been reversed. In this moment of epiphany Louise Kendricks appears in the grove looking "exactly like Bailey" but reminding Maya of Charlotte Brontë's Jane Eyre. Together the two girls explore the possibility of falling into the sky. Holding hands just in case one of them happens to fall in, they lean back in their naturally crafted "easy chairs" and take a "few near tumbles into eternity." Then, in order to intensify the sensation, they move hand in hand to the center of the clearing and begin turning around.

> Very slowly at first. We raised our chins and looked straight at the seductive patch of blue. Faster, just a little faster, then faster, faster yet. Yes, help, we were falling. Then eternity won, after all. We couldn't stop spinning or falling until I was jerked out of her grasp by greedy gravity and thrown to my fate below—no, above, not below. *I found myself* safe and dizzy at the foot of the sycamore tree. Louise had ended on her knees at the other side of the grove. (119, emphasis added)

What this all suggests is that Maya, by choosing *for herself* which path to follow, has indeed *found herself*, "safe and dizzy," but finally on the "path to 'normal' womanhood." She also finds her first female friend.

Together they create a "feminine space" in a private "language" they share but cannot comprehend. They call their language *Tut* and consider it, by virtue of its level of "difficulty," superior to the Pig Latin the other children speak. Despite the ambivalence of its name (it invokes the legendary Egyptian king), *Tut* is for Maya and Louise "the feminine other side" of language, to borrow an expression from Elaine Showalter.[63] *Tut* refuses to signify. It communicates nothing. It conveys no meaning. Yet it is the very impossibility of communication that appeals to the two young girls. *Tut* makes Maya and Louise giggle. And according to Maya, "girls have to giggle, and after being a woman for three years I was about to become a girl" (120). For three years Maya had inhabited an ambiguous, but gender-specific *womanish* space. Now, with her self-imposed silence definitively broken, and with Louise to help negotiate her gender-related affairs, Maya could finally enjoy just being a girl.

4 Seeking the Other Women of (Black) Feminist Literary Critical and Theoretical Discourses

> If I, the black person, can speak freely in my choice of critical
> and creative forms, then my private and collective suffering is
> not only mobilized on my own behalf, but also preserves me
> against the "homicidal" tendencies of strangers.
>
> —Hortense Spillers, "Formalism Comes to Harlem"

The relationship between language and communication and silence and speaking has become an important theme, not only in literature written by black women but in (black) feminist literary criticism and theory as well. Josephine Donovan, in her landmark *Feminist Literary Criticism,* describes feminist criticism as a form of praxis which should, among other things, "enable women—as readers and as writers—to break their culture of silence."[1] Barbara Smith remarks that her groundbreaking essay, "Toward a Black Feminist Criticism," sought to break the "massive silence" imposed on black women writers by the male dominated literary establishment.[2] And more recently, Cheryl Wall has edited an anthology of critical essays by a group of academic critics concerned with making explicit a "positionality" intended to respond to "the false universalism that long defined critical practice and rendered black women and their writing mute."[3]

Most of the essays included in Wall's *Changing Our Own Words* are expanded versions of papers that were presented in 1987 during a symposium on black women writers at Rutgers University. Wall writes that the speakers, all of whom have a "primary professional commitment to black women's writing," were asked to reflect on a number of questions that have to do with developing theories specific to black women's writing. She adds that the "overarching" question of the symposium was "how to bring the terms *criticism, theory,* and *writing by black women* into conjunction" (10).

Valerie Smith attempts such a conjunction in "Black Feminist Theory and the Representation of the 'Other.'" Smith defines black feminist theory as "theory written (or practiced) by black feminists," and as "a way of reading inscriptions of race (particularly but not exclusively blackness), gender (particularly but not exclusively womanhood), and class in modes of cultural expression." Her stated intention in this essay is to "examine black feminism in the context of these related theoretical positions in order to raise questions about the way the 'other' is represented in oppositional discourse." She writes that with the increasing institutionalization of modes of inquiry (feminist literary theory, Afro-Americanist literary theory) that were once considered radical, this kind of questioning seems especially important (39).

Valerie Smith traces the development of black feminist criticism from its earliest stage as a reaction to the "critical acts of omission and condescension" by "white male, Anglo-American feminist, and male Afro-American scholars" to what she calls its present "theoretical phase" (39). She describes the first phase of black feminist criticism as a "first-stage archaeological project" during which writers and critics like Mary Helen Washington, Barbara Smith, and Deborah McDowell undertook a number of editorial projects in order to recover the writings of black women that had been previously either overlooked, ignored, or misread by the literary establishment. This gave way to a second phase in which black feminists were primarily concerned with the close revisionary readings and textual analyses of the African-American literary canon.

According to Valerie Smith, the third stage or "theoretical phase" differs from the two preceding ones in that a number of feminists—she names Susan Willis, Hazel Carby, Mary Helen Washington, Dianne Sandoff, Deborah McDowell, and Hortense Spillers—are more concerned with the ways in which literary study changes "once questions of race, class, and gender become central to the process of literary analysis," than with the "silences in other critical traditions" (46). Valerie Smith argues that these feminists' critical practices involve challenging concepts of literary study that tend to erase, by making the black woman the point of intersection between the experiences of black men and white women, the uniqueness or specificity of the black woman's experience of oppression. She describes the methods of black feminist literary theorists as "necessarily flexible, holding in balance the three variables of race, gender, and class and destabilizing the centrality of any one. More generally, [black feminist literary theorists] call into question a variety of standards of valuation that mainstream feminist and androcentric Afro-Americanist theory might naturalize" (47). Valerie Smith feels that these methods have helped to prevent black feminist literary theory from replicating the totalizing tendencies of "Anglo-American feminism and male Afro-Americanism" (49). Yet she admits that black feminist literary discourse is, for the most part, heterosexual and Afro-American centered. (Only recently, with the intervention of such critical anthologies as *Ngambika* and *Out of the Kumbla*,[4] has black feminist literary discourse begun to broaden its scope to include African and Black diaspora literature.)

Black feminist literary discourse is also a discourse of privilege, a purely academic discourse, as Barbara Christian reminds us when she asks in "The State of Black Feminist Criticism(s)," "Does our emphasis on definitions and theories mean that we will close ourselves to those, the many, who know or care little about the intense debates that take so much of our time in universities? Can we conceive of our literary critical activities as related to the activism necessary to substantively change black women's lives?"[5] To these questions I would like to add the following: Does not the race, class, gender formulation of black feminist discourse in fact imply an "actual" or potentially totalizing universal value (indeed a universal subject) with which all other black women involved in literary critical activities *must* identify? If so, does not black feminism risk practicing its own forms of exclusion by censoring—*silencing*—those feminine voices that, for whatever reasons, do not adequately adhere to this new holy trinity? In other words, who speaks for the other women of (black) literary critical and theoretical discourse?

One of the most dramatic demonstrations of the implications of this last question for many feminist critics and theorists is offered by Elaine Showalter in "A Criticism of Our Own: Autonomy and Assimilation in Afro-American and Feminist Literary Theory." Showalter recalls having participated in a 1985 conference on literary theory at Georgetown University where a young woman had been hired to translate all of the papers into sign language for the hearing impaired. What Showalter found most troubling about this otherwise not so unusual academic arrangement was that neither the "distinguished Marxist theorist" who had taken over the podium on the first day of the conference nor the two white male theorists who spoke after him acknowledged the presence of the graceful young woman standing only a few feet away from them. "No one introduced her; no one alluded to her. It was as if they could not see her. She had become transparent, like the female medium of the symbolists who, according to Mary Ann Caws, 'served up the sign, conveying it with fidelity, patience, and absolute personal silence. She herself was patiently ruled out.'"[6]

As this "guerilla theater of sexual difference"[7] continued throughout the morning, Showalter began to wonder how she, the fourth theorist and the first woman to speak, would reconcile her "position of power"—and her language—with her identification with "the silent, transparent woman" who represented for her not only the "feminine other side of discourse," but the "Other Woman of feminist discourse" as well: "the woman outside of academia in the "real world," or the Third World, to whom a Feminist critic is responsible, just as she is responsible to the standards and conventions of criticism."[8]

What Showalter seems to have overlooked is that the translator was as much a part of academia and its discourses as the theorists themselves. Like the intellectuals (or the experts, depending on how you define these terms) who had gathered together to exchange information and presumably to engage in meaningful discussions, the translator had been deployed to further the interests of literary theory. Her task was to render accessible to hearing impaired participants the discourses that helped to structure this particular event. Consequently, the woman in the real world, to whom Showalter claims the feminist critic is responsible, remained unaccounted for. She was not invited because, unlike the translator, she neither speaks nor signs the specialized language of literary theory. Yet Showalter, with a beneficence symptomatic of a *ma*tronizing attitude, reiterates Gayatri Spivak's concern that the (uninvited) other woman at least be acknowledged by academic feminism[9] without taking into consideration the fact that Spivak insists upon something much more crucial than mere acknowledgement or recognition of women in the "real world."

In "French Feminism in an International Frame," Spivak argues for a "simultaneous other focus" of academic feminism that would call into question the complex relationship between the feminist investigator and her "colonized" subject whose response to the feminist project is often at best one of amused tolerance.

I see no way to avoid insisting that there has to be a simultaneous other focus: not merely who am I? But who is the other woman? How am I naming her? How does she name me? Is this part of the problematic I discuss? Indeed, it is the absence of such unfeasible but crucial questions that makes the "colonized woman" as "subject" see the investigators as sweet and sympathetic creatures from another planet who are free to come and go; or, depending on her own socialization in the colonizing cultures, see "feminism" as having a vanguardist class fix, the liberties it fights for as luxuries, finally identifiable with "free sex" of one kind or another.[10]

Once Showalter and the other women at the conference became aware of the "Other Woman," they acknowledged her by introducing her and by changing their lectures "in order to work with her presence."[11] These "sympathetic" gestures were certainly well intentioned, but they hardly address what Spivak calls the discontinuity between "infinitely privileged" female academics as investigators *and* subjects and women in the Third World. Neither do they precipitate the kind of self-scrutiny Spivak insists is necessary if the other women of feminist discourse are to see feminism as something other than the frivolous activities of "infinitely privileged" academic women. In fact, what Showalter shows is that many academic feminists, as they struggle to meet the demands of their profession, remain oblivious to the presence of the "Other Woman." In many instances, they only become aware of her *after* she has gained access to the academy, as in the case of Showalter's translator or in my own peculiar situation as a high school drop-out, unmarried teenage parent, welfare recipient, domestic, chambermaid, waitress, et cetera, et cetera, and so forth, who now holds a Ph.D. and a faculty position in a Big Ten university. The truly dispossessed rarely, if ever, catch a glimpse of the academics, black or white, female or male, who claim to speak on our behalf. University professors simply do not, for the most part, venture that deeply into the "real world."

For feminist critics and others who work within so-called "oppositional discourses," the lacunae separating academia from the "real world" create a double bind, as Showalter has pointed out. For African and black diaspora feminist literary critics, this double bind is redoubled as a result of their "double allegiance" to feminism and to the liberation of all African peoples. Carole Boyce Davies describes this double allegiance in her introduction to *Ngambika:*

On the one hand there is a grounding in the need to liberate African peoples from neo-colonialism and other forms of race and class oppression, coupled with a respect for certain features of traditional African cultures. On the other, there is the influence of the international woman's movement and the recognition that a feminist consciousness is necessary in examining the position of women in African societies. The tension involved in this double allegiance provides a nexus from which this criticism grows.[12]

Sometimes the tension involved in this double allegiance erupts into full blown conflicts between black women and black men. To cite just one example, during the University of Wisconsin-Madison's 1991 "Afro-American Studies in the Twenty-First Century" conference, Hazel Carby led what a local weekly Madison newspaper called a "feminist revolt" against black male intellectuals whom she criticized for having marginalized black feminists. The primary target of her attack was Houston Baker, whom she severely castigated for not including Black feminism in the paper he presented on the "Afro-American Studies and Ethnic Studies" panel. Carby accused her black male colleagues of having reduced the role of black female critics to that of "the superfluous adornments needed to bolster the male critical ego," and of treating them like "intellectual concubines." According to one journalist, her speech, which ended with an unequivocal demand for equality, was greeted with a roar and a standing ovation from the crowd.

> "We are your intellectual equals. Treat us like it," Carby demanded. With that, she stepped away from the podium. The crowd roared and gave her a standing ovation.
> That speech summed up a deep-seated tension that runs throughout African-American studies—what Nellie McKay calls "the quarrel between the brothers and the sisters."[13]

The stakes are obviously very high for black American feminist literary critics. According to McKay, many of them feel that male "stars" (a term used to define prominent university professors that *reeks* of Hollywood's sleazy glamour and glitz) like Baker and Henry Louis Gates, Jr., have taken over the movement initiated by black feminists "without using feminist insights."[14] It is not my intention to debate whether or not Baker and Gates have taken over the black feminist movement. Given the strong ideological (race-class-gender) imperatives that power the movement's machinations, I doubt that such a takeover is possible. Neither am I concerned with whether or not they have used feminist insights. I leave those issues for others to debate and decide. What I would like to point out is that a number of African and black diaspora feminist literary critics, in an effort to avoid the kinds of antagonisms that presently exist between the "brothers and sisters," have tried to redefine feminism through critical approaches that do not always respect the balance that Valerie Smith feels holds the race-class-gender variables in check. For instance, Carole Boyce Davies chose Filomina Steady's introduction to *The Black Woman Cross-Culturally* [15] as the starting point for her discussion of African feminism in *Ngambika*. Davies feels that despite its shortcomings (it glosses too quickly over "certain traditional inequities that continue to subordinate African women" [16]), Steady's cross-cultural approach to feminism [17] offers important insights into the socioeconomic and class factors that contribute to black women's oppression (*Ngambika* 7).

Steady, an anthropologist who was born in Sierra Leone, argues that the "accusation of *universal* male oppression through the system of patriarchy has been politically advantageous to white women" and to those upwardly mobile black women who might be inclined to form allegiances with feminist rather than racial causes because they find the latter too provocative to serve their individual interests within the white power structure (*WiA* 3, emphasis added). She writes that since it is the poor black woman rather than the "mythical Atlas" who holds up "our unequal and unjust planet," a theory of African feminism must combine "racial, sexual, class, and cultural dimensions of oppression" from a perspective that defines women as human rather than merely sexual beings (*WiA* 4). The shift, then, would be from the kinds of male/female polarizations that define most Western, including black American feminism(s), to the very fundamental issue of survival that, according to Steady, has always been crucial for African (and I might add, poor black American) women. Steady argues that African feminism must organize itself around parallel masculine/feminine concepts of autonomy, communalism, and cooperation rather than the notions of dichotomy, individualism, competition, and opposition that characterize Western feminism since what is at stake for most Africans, and for most people who constitute the so-called Third World, is opposition to the structures of oppression that seek to reduce all "colonial subjects," female and male, to a kind of standing reserve—raw material for American and European exploitation. Steady describes "African patterns of feminism" as having developed from a view of human life that does not constitute the male (or the female, for that matter) as the other. "Each gender constitutes the critical half that makes the human whole. Neither sex is totally complete in itself to constitute a unit by itself. Each has and needs a complement,[18] despite the possession of unique features of its own" (*WiA* 8).

Steady does not deny that this complementarity is for the most part unequal. African urbanization, unfair labor practices and unequal access to formal education, among other things, continue to place black women among "the most vulnerable victims of poverty" (*WiA* 13–15). Her point, in "African Feminism: a Worldwide Perspective," and in *The Black Woman Cross-Culturally,* is that racism is a major obstacle in black women's struggles to acquire their basic needs. Therefore, what is required is a more rigorous analysis of the "racial factor" and its relationship to class and sex inequalities than has been undertaken by current theoretical approaches to feminist studies that tend to emphasize gender differences instead (*WiA* 19). Steady proposes a humanist feminism organized around the idea that male/female complementarity is necessary for "ensuring the totality of human existence within a balanced ecosystem," and for eradicating oppression in all of its manifestations. Her global perspective on African feminism as a form of social action places black women at the center of this emancipatory project because African women have always been involved in the struggle for liberation from all forms of oppression, including race and class oppression (*WiA* 21–22).

Carole Boyce Davies derives her notion of a "genuine African feminism" from Steady's anthropological investigations and from the insights of African women writers and critics like Omolara Ogundipe-Leslie, Gwendolyn Konie, and Annabella Rodrigues, a Mozambican who was active in the FRELIMO liberation movement.

A "genuine African feminism" as Davies articulates it in *Ngambika* is based on seven assumptions that are inextricably bound to the social and political realities of contemporary African society.[19] First and foremost is the fact that while African feminism challenges African men to be aware of the extent to which they participate in the subjugation of women, it is not antagonistic toward them since it recognizes that both African men and women must engage in a common struggle against European and American imperialism. Second, while African feminism acknowledges certain affinities with international feminism, the "African feminist consciousness" delineates needs and goals that are specific to African women living in African societies. Third, the historical perspective of African feminism must recognize the precolonial social structures in which female participation was equal to and often exceeded that of men. The fourth point deals with the sensitive issues of obligatory motherhood and polygamy and the attempts by some African feminists—Buchi Emecheta is an example—to examine these problems from an African rather than a Western perspective. The fifth and sixth points concern "African women's self-reliance, and the role they must play in postindependence reconstruction. The final point made by Davies is the one that speaks most directly to the objectives of *Ngambika:* specifically, "the traditional and contemporary avenues of choice" for African women must be defined by African women themselves. In other words, to restate the imperative implicit in Davies' assessment of African feminism, African women must continue to "tell their own stories" (*Ngambika* 8–10). As literary critics, their task is "to identify critical approaches and standards and criteria which have been applied so far to the study of African literature from a feminist perspective and which can be utilized and built upon for further examination of women in/and African literature" (*Ngambika* 12).

Interestingly, while Davies is strongly optimistic about recent developments in African feminism and African feminist literary discourse, she feels that feminism in the Caribbean environment has been slow to generate "sufficient excitement and passion," especially among Caribbean intellectuals and activists. In a dialogue with Elaine Savory Fido, Davies hypothesizes that Caribbean feminism and feminist literary discourse lack "strong, committed argument" about feminist issues because, unlike many African societies, Caribbean societies are not presently "struggling through questions of liberation," questions that cannot ignore the relationship between "women's emancipation" and "total liberation."[20] I would argue that, on the contrary, it is precisely because many Caribbean societies are struggling for total liberation, and Haiti is the most recent example of this, that feminist issues have not garnered the kind of support they have received from the more developed countries. I don't think it is unreasonable to suggest that, in most cases, the overwhelming social, political, and economic problems with which the majority of the people living in the Caribbean environment must deal as a matter of course would most certainly supersede the problems that occupy academic feminists.

Elaine Savory Fido proposes another explanation for the apparent lack of support for feminist issues in the Caribbean that casts feminism in such religious overtones that one wonders if the appropriate gesture wouldn't be to genuflect. "Like any movement with integrity, it requires that a person live her/his life *entirely* by its principles, and not many are prepared to go that far at this stage, especially in the Caribbean where small societies exert tremendous pressure for conformity on the individual" (*Kumbla* xi, emphasis added). It requires that one "leave" one's former life and become a "fallible follower" of the principles of feminism that would now provide the moral and ethical guidelines for one's life.

"Fallible followers" is what Elizabeth Struthers Malbon calls the followers of Jesus as they are represented in the Gospel of Mark. They are called "fallible" because their call to repentance is based on what is *understood* in the Gospel to be the tensions between their success and failure, as disciples, to live "according to the behavior demanded by Jesus."[21] One could say that the Gospel of Mark attempts to raise the implied reader's consciousness about followership in order to encourage personal change. Similarly feminism, especially in the early stages of its development, placed a great deal of emphasis on consciousness-raising and on the Gospel—on *spreading the word* about the "CR process" as a first step toward encouraging "the 'personal change' that makes political transformation and action possible."[22] Thus "followership," and this is something that Fido obviously has not considered, whether it be that of Jesus or feminism or any other powerful ideology, likewise demands conformity. It demands conformity to and faith in an undisputed ideal.

For black feminist literary critics, "followership" also demands a belief that literature and criticism are somehow empowered to transform the lives of black women despite the fact that the high levels of illiteracy among black women in the United States, Africa, and the Caribbean environment suggest that it will take more than a few good books to change the conditions under which they struggle to survive. In "Words Whispered Over Voids," the Ghanaian poet and critic Abena Busia writes that "it is in the belief that our narratives can be transformational that we begin."[23] This transformation involves a "rebellious process of self-definition and redefinition" in the fiction of black women writers that, according to Busia, must first be understood in terms of a very specific "political and ideological context," a context circumscribed by their situation as black women struggling to define themselves in their own terms within the "prisonhouses" of their academies. "As black women we live and work against odds we all know. In the first place, we are women. This is not the place to fight over again the question of what it is that makes women and women's literature different. We embrace the faith that the feminist movement has established our right to talk about our selves in our own terms, and we need no other explanation."[24] Yet despite her *faith* in the feminist movement—the word faith appears no less than four times in this essay, Busia shares the opinion of most black feminists that feminism has not adequately addressed issues concerning black women. Therefore, in her attempt to define a criticism specific to the "collective narratives" of black diaspora women writers, she finds it necessary to turn to Alice Walker's *womanism* in order to distinguish the critical practices of black women from those of white women. She writes that the word *feminist* "has come to mean, within the academy, the study of white women. Hence the need for a different word: If we do not find words for ourselves, we will be lost."[25] Womanism, then, is to be the new saving grace for the black woman writer. Or, to put it in the words of Chikwenye Ogunyemi, a Nigerian *womanist* writer, "Womanism with its wholesome, its religious grounding in black togetherness, is her *gospel* of hope."[26]

Ogunyemi, who claims to have derived her "womanist aesthetic" independently of Alice Walker, describes womanism as

> a philosophy that celebrates black roots, the ideals of black life, while giving a balanced presentation of black womandom. It concerns itself as much with the black sexual power tussle as with the world power structure that subjugates blacks. Its ideal is for black unity where every black person has a modicum of power and so can be a "brother" or "sister" or a "father" or a "mother" to the other. This philosophy has a mandalic core: its aim is the dynamism of wholeness and self-healing that one sees in the positive, integrative endings of womanist novels.[27]

While few people would disagree with the womanist ideal as Ogunyemi articulates it, there are certain aspects of her womanist philosophy that Western trained black feminists and womanists would find problematic, to say the least. One has to do with her treatment of the theme of the "gifted" woman in relation to polygamy in African literature. Ogunyemi argues that what Maryse Condé calls the "deep-rooted conflict" that writers like Flora Nwapa and Ama Ata Aidoo express in their early novels, through their portrayal and destruction of the "gifted woman" who cannot find a suitable mate, can be attributed to the influence of white feminism on their thinking and writing. "I suggest that this problem partly arises from the fact that early in their careers the African writers tend to model themselves on white feminists, thus putting themselves at variance with polygamy, which is generally accepted in rural Africa and is gaining ground in urban Nigeria."[28]

Ogunyemi refers to Mariama Bâ's *So Long a Letter* as a novel that successfully explores the problem of polygamy from an African rather than a Western perspective. She feels that Bâ's presentation of Ramatoulaye as a "determined heroine" who is able to finally reconcile herself to the "libidinous disposition" of Fulani men is an example of "womanism in action." "The demands of Fulani culture rather than those of sexual politics predominate. Though [Ramatoulaye] recognizes the inequities of patriarchy, she never really fights for her 'rights'—a position further expressed by the novel's epistolary form."[29] Needless to say, Ogunyemi's position is extreme. No matter what one's perspective, polygamy presents a major obstacle to the development of modern African societies. This is what Mariama Bâ skillfully conveys in her novel, which ends with Ramatoulaye fighting for her "rights" by rejecting the man who would, in traditional Fulani society, become her second husband after her first husband's death. In this sense, then, Ogunyemi misreads the novel. "Womanism in action" in *So Long a Letter* has less to do with Ramatoulaye reconciling herself to the "libidinous disposition of Fulani men" than with challenging the basic assumptions of polygamy in an increasingly urbanized African, or more specifically, Senegalese society.

Nancy Morejón, who C. Rose Green-Williams describes as "the leading black female poet writing in contemporary Cuba,"[30] shares Ogunyemi's concern about the influence of feminism on the cultures of "underdeveloped countries." In an interview with Elaine Savory Fido, Morejón insists that she does not speak as a feminist although she respects certain feminist movements, especially Alice Walker's version of womanism. The problem as she sees it is that these movements have more to do with a consumer society than with issues that take into account the society and history of the countries that constitute the Caribbean region. "They develop ideas that belong maybe best to a consumer society. I think the task of a womanist (let's talk with Alice Walker's term which I love very much) in our region should be something related to our society and to our history. We cannot import certain patterns of these movements from Western Europe or developed countries because we are underdeveloped countries" (*Kumbla* 267). Morejón goes on to explain that although much of her poetry strongly relates to women, she does not think just in terms of a woman's culture. Her concern is with a "mixed culture" where the

relations between men and women must be worked out without the "arti-
ficial tensions" created by the intervention of "these naïve movements"
(*Kumbla* 266). Moreover, Morejón reminds Fido that as a poet she is concerned with beauty and with teaching people to see beauty as part of their
concrete reality rather than with something that exists as a mere abstrac-
tion.[31] What she calls the Cuban woman writer's "womanist condition"
includes white women and is just one aspect of an increasingly mature
"national expression" (*Kumbla* 268).

This strong emphasis on culture as opposed to sexual politics is one
reason Carole Boyce Davies and Elaine Savory Fido, in their dialogue on
Caribbean feminism, deal with womanism as a "cultural manifestation"
of feminism. They both agree that womanism is more sensitive to experiences other than those of Western white women. However, they do
not believe that it is as ideologically sound as the various adjectival forms
of feminism—*radical* feminism, *Marxist* feminism, *Black* feminism—or
Patricia McFadden's "woman consciousness," a term they feel is an "important redefinition of feminism in a third world context" (*Kumbla*, xii).

Within the domain of literary criticism, Fido feels that some notions
of womanism, particularly Ogunyemi's, are "too rejecting of feminism to
be sensitive to the literature" that is the subject of womanist discourse.
(Kumbla, xii). Hence Fido's insistence on connecting the word womanism, with a slash, to its correlative term, *feminism*. Womanism is the quali-
fier that inscribes the variable of race onto the discourse of feminism. It
signals what Sylvia Wynter in the "Afterward" to *Out of the Kumbla* has
called the "contradictory dualism" and "cross-roads situation" of Caribbean women writers and critics who use the "still essentially Western discourse of feminism" in an effort to move "towards a new post-modern
and post-Western mode of cognitive inquiry" (*Kumbla* 356).

Wynter refers to the German scholar Hans Blumenberg's expansion
of Thomas Kuhn's theory of "scientific revolutions" to support her argument that the contradiction implicit in the insertion of the variable *race*
into the discourse of feminism, as exemplified in the essays included in
the anthology, will finally precipitate a downfall of " 'our present school
like mode of thought' " in much the same way that the variable *gender* has
presumably destabilized the " 'universal' theories of Liberal Humanism
and Marxism-Leninism" (*Kumbla* 357). The variable *race*, as it is encoded
in the term "womanist" as Alice Walker defines it, has most certainly
called into question any notion of a universal theory of feminism.[32] But
I would argue that rather than pointing toward the "emergent downfall"

of our present " 'school like mode of thought,' " the contradiction that places the womanist/feminist writer/critic in her "cross-roads situation" has merely helped to replace that mode of thought with *ideological thinking*. In some ways, ideological thinking is much more insidious since it limits the possibilities for any kind of *thinking* to occur in the first place. One need only look at recent developments on college and university campuses in the United States to see the extent to which the ideology of feminism in its various guises is developing into what Hannah Arendt would call an "obligatory pattern of thought" not only for literary study, but for all of the Humanities, the Social Sciences and even the so-called pure sciences as well.

Hannah Arendt is an *Other* woman whose work has been, until recently, ignored by feminist theorists of all stripes. Maria Markus attributes this apparent lack of interest in Arendt to what she calls a "disturbing tendency" in feminist theory to "persistently ignore women thinkers unless they openly declare their allegiance to feminism."[33] Markus writes that this problematic demand for "loyalty" is not only "dangerously self-limiting" and "inconsistent with feminist theory." It also risks impoverishing feminist theory by depriving it of the valuable "new" perspectives that works by serious thinkers like Arendt can contribute.

Arendt's definition of ideology and ideological thinking in relation to two of the three variables, racism and classism, of womanist/feminist discourse can certainly offer a different, if not new, perspective on the implications of this ideology for the study of African, Afro-American, and Caribbean literature. It must be kept in mind, however, that the frame of reference for Arendt's analyses of these two variables in *The Origins of Totalitarianism* is Eastern and Western Europe. Her emphasis is on Nazi Germany, although she also gives a detailed account of how the ideology of racism and the organizing principles of bureaucracy were essential for maintaining the transatlantic slave trade and for justifying the expansion of European imperialism.

In *The Origins of Totalitarianism,* Arendt defines ideologies in terms of their ability to attract, persuade, and lead a majority of people "through the various experiences and situations of an average modern life." While the systems of a given ideology may be based on a single opinion, ideology differs from a simple opinion to the extent that "it claims to possess either the key to history, or the solution for all the 'riddles of the universe,' or the intimate knowledge of the hidden laws which are supposed to rule nature and man."[34]

Arendt argues that only two ideologies, the ideology of race and the ideology of class (to which I would add a third, the ideology of gender), have been able to survive the "hard competitive struggle of persuasion" and appeal to such large masses of people that "they were able to enlist state support and establish themselves as official national doctrines. But far beyond the boundaries within which race-thinking and class-thinking have developed into obligatory patterns of thought, free public opinion has adopted them to such an extent that not only intellectuals but great masses of people will no longer accept a presentation of past or present fact that is not in agreement with either of these views" (159).

The ideology of gender has a very long way to go before it will become an "official national doctrine." But now that the study of gender issues has become imperative for students in a number of major colleges and universities, and a feminist perspective is becoming an increasingly important consideration in academic hires,[35] one cannot help but wonder if "gender-thinking," like "race-thinking" and "class-thinking" will soon reveal itself as containing those "totalitarian elements" that Arendt feels are common to all "full-fledged" ideologies.

According to Arendt, ideologies, or the phenomenon of explaining "everything and every occurrence by deducing it from a single premise," did not play a significant role in political life before Hitler and Stalin who discovered their "great political potentialities" (468). The term itself, *ideology,* implies that an idea, be it the idea of god in Deism or the idea of race in racism, can be treated in a scientific manner. But what Arendt argues is that the ideas of ideologies never form the subject matter of the ideologies themselves; nor do they make scientific statements. Ideology means the "logic of an idea." It takes as its subject matter history, "to which the 'idea' is applied:"

> the result of this application is not a body of statements about something that *is,* but the unfolding of a process which is in constant change. . . .
>
> Ideologies are never interested in the miracle of being. They are historical, concerned with becoming and perishing, with the rise and fall of cultures, even if they try to explain history by some "law of nature." The word "race" in racism does not signify any genuine curiosity about the human races as a field for scientific exploration, but is the "idea" by which the movement of history is explained as one consistent process. (469)

Similarly, if we accept Arendt's argument, the word "gender," which is inherent in the ideologies of feminism, does not, particularly in literary studies, signify any genuine curiosity about the being of woman or of literature as such since everything is interpreted, explained, and comprehended from one single premise: that within the realms of the real *and* the fictive, all men are inescapably implicated in the oppression of women. Philosophical thought, with its "necessary insecurity," gets exchanged for the "total explanation" of the ideology. Arendt insists that the danger of comprehending everything in terms of a single premise that has been arrived at through a "consistent process of logical deductions," is not so much "the risk of falling for some usually vulgar, always uncritical assumptions as of exchanging the *freedom* inherent in man's capacity to *think* for the straightjacket of logic" (470, emphasis added). Or of exchanging the freedom to choose one's own creative and critical forms for conformity with paradigms and modes of expression prescribed by whatever ideology happens to prevail.

Ideology's claim to total explanation of the past, "total knowledge of the present," and a "reliable prediction of the future" is the first of what Arendt calls its "totalitarian elements." The second element has to do with the capacity of ideological thinking to become independent of our perceived reality and "insist on a " 'truer' reality concealed behind all perceptible things," about which we can only become aware through a "sixth sense." In totalitarian movements, this sixth sense is provided by the particular ideological indoctrination of education institutions like the Nazi *Ordensburgen* or the schools of the Comintern and Cominform, which were established exclusively for training "political soldiers." The consequences of this kind of training provided by totalitarian movements is that "the propaganda . . . also serves to emancipate thought from experience and reality; it always strives to inject a secret meaning into every public, tangible event and to suspect a secret intent behind every public political act. Once the movements have come to power, they proceed to change reality in accordance with their ideological claims" (470–71).

Ideology's third totalitarian element, as Arendt defines it, has to do with how ideology can only "achieve this emancipation of thought through certain methods of demonstration," the most important of which is the ordering of facts "into an absolutely logical procedure which starts from an axiomatically accepted premise," and produces "everything else from it; that is, it proceeds with a consistency that exists nowhere in the realm of reality" (471). Or, to paraphrase the poet Nikki Giovanni, who deals with the problem of consistency in a slightly different context, if there are no inconsistencies in the world, no contradictions, there can be no thought since consistency is the "hobgoblin of little minds."[36]

Lest my *intention* in invoking Arendt be seriously misunderstood, let me say that I do not mean to suggest an analogy between feminism and the forms of fascism that influenced the politics of the first half of the twentieth century. The points I am trying to make through Arendt's examples are (1) that ideological thinking is incompatible with thinking as a free activity; and (2) that within the Humanities certain *elements* of totalitarianism inhabiting the ideology of gender and its critical practices often operationalize the very kinds of repression/oppression it claims, in theory, to attempt to eradicate. Jean Elshtain, who teaches political science at Vanderbilt University, comments on this by citing the example of a female philosopher who was "attacked" by feminists (Elshtain doesn't say which feminists) because they didn't approve of her "scholarly enthusiasm" for St. Augustine. "She was told, in no uncertain terms, that a woman had no business reading and writing about a person who, after all, had some very strange views. It is odd and unfortunate that in the name of feminism this kind of retreat is occurring and that people are not being freed up to roam as they will and to explore as they might."[37]

Needless to say, there are many serious feminist scholars and writers, female and male, who condemn these kinds of attacks. But this atmosphere of intolerance often places "non-feminists" and women writers and critics who, for whatever reasons, do not hold strong feminist convictions, on the defensive about issues that have little or nothing to do with literature. For instance, in 1986 Maya Angelou was confronted about her "convictions" during an interview with Aminatta Forna who had visited her in her London hotel ostensibly to talk about *The Heart of a Woman*, the fourth volume of Angelou's autobiography. Forna, who describes the incident in an article entitled, ironically, "Kicking Ass," objected to Angelou's treatment in the text of her relationship with Vusumzi Make. Ignoring Angelou's clever uses of irony and parody, especially in the episodes dealing with Make, Forna complains that Angelou "wrote at length" about how she tried to become a "good African wife" to the South African freedom fighter.

I found this infuriating, and since the fifth volume *All God's Children Need Traveling Shoes* won't be published until 1987, *I was curious to know whether she deserved her brilliant reputation.*

Ms. Angelou, I asked her, do you now consider yourself a feminist? Her eyes almost gave off sparks. "What do you mean, do I consider myself a feminist? I am a feminist. I've been female for a long time now. I'd be stupid not to be on my own side.

In self-defense, I replied that this did not always seem to have been the case.[38]

Aminatta Forna learned quickly what the rest of us already know—that Maya Angelou "don't take no stuff offa nobody," to put it in the vernacular. Yet this incident, as Forna reports it, raises certain issues for (black) feminism and literary criticism that need to be addressed. One concern, which I briefly touched on in the previous chapter, has to do with the relationship between the writer's personal and political convictions and what is represented in her writing, or the problematic of the "voice."

Roland Barthes has insisted that this relationship is marked by the disappearance or death of the author as the originator of a single subject who speaks in a unified voice. Michel Foucault expands upon Barthes by installing in the space vacated by the now defunct author what he calls the "author function." This "author function" disperses the speaking subject throughout the discursive field of the text as a multiplicity of voices that, by virtue of their tasks or functions, cannot be reduced to the "figure of the author."[39] The subject is therefore "deprived" (or perhaps relieved) of its traditional role as the organizing principle of a literary text while the text is presumably "liberated" from the hegemony of authorial privilege and the abiding question, "Who is speaking anyway, and what difference does it make?" Most writers and critics readily concede that to equate the author with the voice that "speaks" in the text is to commit a serious act of misreading. But an increasing number of both writers and critics object to what they feel is an effort, in the wake of post-structuralism, to erase the author or what the feminist critic Cheryl Walker refers to as "author recognition" from the text at the very moment when previously marginalized writers have begun to assert themselves as critical voices on the literary scene.

In "Feminist Literary Criticism and the Author,"[40] Walker surveys a number of recent feminist critical works that take up the problem of authorship. She settles on Cora Kaplan's *Sea Changes* as the paradigmatic text for her own assumptions about who's speaking and the difference it makes. Walker admits that Kaplan, who is a feminist Marxist critic, does not "specifically address the idea of the death of the author." Instead,

Kaplan's analyses of writers and critics like Ellen Moers, Anne Sexton, and Elizabeth Barrett Browning suggest a reconsideration of "author function" in relation to these women's "actual" experiences in history, according to Walker (565).

Walker lists five "essential components" of Kaplan's view of authorship that she feels can be useful in formulating a feminist response to Foucault's (and Beckett's) question about who is speaking. Components one and two state simply that literary texts have authors, but that the "fluid nature of subjectivity" prevents them from becoming "full subjective presences" in their texts. Number three has to do with the usefulness of psychoanalysis and sociopolitical criticism in bringing the "author's experience in culture" to bear upon the text without reducing the text to such interpretations. Number four describes one of criticism's important functions as that of ideology's *overseer:* "to see how ideology emerges in the context of a specific historical text *or* subjectivity, which is simultaneously social and psychic." The fifth component rejects Barthes's "so-called hypostases (author, society, history, psyche)" as "unified or totalizing in their effects" and asserts that all we have to do to more clearly understand the "complexity of culture and psyche" is read more literary texts (566)!

Based on these five components, it is difficult to see how Kaplan's ideas about authorship differ substantially from those that preceded the radical intervention of structuralism and post-structuralism. Yet Walker insists that Kaplan's "implicit dialogue with Barthes and Foucault" offers her the necessary middle ground or "site" from which she can formulate her own "theoretical response to Foucault's question" (566). Walker agrees with Barthes's and Foucault's assertions that the author as a "specific historical subjectivity" is not the determining factor of a literary text (567). But she cannot accept the pervasiveness of the *masculine pronoun* in Barthes's "short and pithy" essay and Foucault's expansion of it. Walker questions what she feels is Barthes's impersonality on the grounds that the "generic masculine pronouns" that proliferate his "abstract formulations" and his "linguistic practice" obscure the "differences among writers and readers" (568–69). As for Foucault, Walker takes issue with his remark in "What is an Author" about how the writer, as he writes, cancels out the signs of his particular individuality and in the singularity of his own absence must "'assume the role of the dead man in the game of writing.'" Walker's question is, "Does this work equally well with all writers? Here it seems to me the difference between writing subjectivities is crucial. For H. D., for instance, writing does not place her in the position of the dead man for 'she herself is the writing,' as she said in one work, and the choice for her is to 'write, write or die,' not to write *and* die, as Foucault says is now customary" (569).

Obviously Walker, like many feminist critics, reads Barthes's and Foucault's pronouns literally. And it is precisely this literal reading that weakens her argument. After having pointed out the shortcomings of some of the most influential feminist critical responses to the death of the author, Walker reduces her own inquest to a problem in grammar. In the end, it is the pervasiveness of the pronoun *he* in Barthes and Foucault that prompts Walker to propose a brand of *"persona criticism"* that would reinstate the author, who now wears a mask bearing many "social configurations," as something more than an "abstract indeterminacy" that has no being outside of the text. A leftist politics and ideology would return to govern our reading/rewriting of literary texts so that "previously obscure dimensions of women's history and women's relation to language, authorship, creativity, identity" can finally be illuminated (571). In other words, Walker's brand of *"persona criticism"* would reinstate the "old-fashioned assumptions" other feminists have tried to move away from. But this time, those assumptions will be wearing the guise of *difference*. Walker's response to Foucault's question is "the difference it makes, in terms of the voices I can persuade you are speaking, occupies a crucial position in the ongoing discussion of difference itself " (571).

Equally important for many feminists involved in this "ongoing discussion of difference" is how a writer defines herself in relation to the feminist project. Among the questions this discussion raises for the other women of literary discourse is, Does a woman writer or critic have to *call* herself a feminist or womanist in order to be "on her own side?" Is Gayl Jones, who does not identify herself as a feminist any less committed to women's issues than women writers who do? Also, what are the bases for (black) feminist critical judgments of women's literature? What authorizes some women writers to arrogantly assert what other women writers' convictions should be? Who or what has empowered some women writers/critics to question whether or not other women writers/critics *deserve* their "brilliant reputations?"

One thing Valerie Smith makes clear in her attempt to confront some of these problems is that a lot depends on the "political and professional returns" one can expect from investing in the (black) feminist literary and critical project. In "Gender and Afro-Americanist Literary Theory and Criticism," Smith writes that the work of recent black feminists is concerned primarily with "developing ways of reading and talking about figurations of race and gender" in the "literary and cultural productions" of black women. This work proceeds from the assumption that the "conditions of oppression provide the subtext of all Afro-Americanist literary criticism and theory. Whether a critic/theorist explores representations of the experience of oppression or strategies by which that experience is transformed, he/she assumes the existence of an 'other' against whom/which blacks struggle."[41]

In what Valerie Smith calls the "classic tradition of Afro-Americanist criticism and theory," the "oppressive 'other'" has always been seen as "a figure of white power" and never as a figure of black male authority. Gender issues were dealt with in one of the following three ways, according to Valerie Smith: "in a biographical framework permeated by sexual stereotypes of women; in assertions of male authority within the Black Arts movement; and in an ostensibly gender-blind literary history that did not give equal weight to women's texts."[42]

Smith turns to Darwin Turner's *In a Minor Chord* to show how one black male critic used the biographical approach to enhance the literary careers of his black male subjects, Jean Toomer and Countee Cullen, and to denigrate that of his black female subject, Zora Neale Hurston. She criticizes Turner for beginning his chapters on Toomer and Cullen by first establishing their "literary power" and then moving on to a biographical reading of their careers without suggesting ways in which their "relation to constructions of masculinity figure in their writing." Valerie Smith argues that, in the chapter on Hurston, Turner does the opposite. "Instead of establishing her literary power, Turner opens the chapter with an extended examination of her personal eccentricities. Drawing from her autobiography and recollections of her foes and associates alike, he devotes the first third of this chapter to creating an image of Hurston as one who was indifferent to her own and other blacks' dignity, obsequious to whites, opportunistic, and politically retrograde."[43]

Part of the black feminist project involves challenging these male biases through a radical rereading of black women's literature that strongly emphasizes how gender affects one's critical judgment. Hence, while Turner reads Janie's speech to Jody in the deathbed scene in *Their Eyes Were Watching God* as the cruel conduct of a vindictive woman, and one of the "crudest scenes" Hurston ever wrote, it is generally acclaimed by feminists as "a victory for a woman denied her right to speak for herself and in her own voice."[44] In both instances, ideology displaces aesthetics as the criteria for critical judgment. Literary merit is obviously secondary to the race or gender dispute.[45] In the case of the latter, the gender issue has indeed been victorious: the general consensus is that Zora Neale Hurston is a *great* novelist, and woe-be-it unto anyone who dares to think otherwise (although I would like to humbly submit that Hurston's "feminism" is much more strongly articulated and cleverly rendered in Part 1 of *Tell My Horse*).[46]

Valerie Smith remarks in her overview of the Black Arts movement and the reconstructionist period of the late 1970s and early 1980s that black feminists have forced a reconsideration of the black woman's (prone) position through their impressive bibliographical and editorial projects. They have also "gendered the discourse of Afro-Americanist theory by *writing specifically as women*"; that is, their writing challenges "the boundaries that traditionally have separated personal, political, and theoretical writing, boundaries that support a hierarchy that has always excluded black women's cultural productions." As a form of "self-inscription," their writing involves a "process of tradition-building" that "provides them with intellectual and political antecedents."[47] Interestingly, the "politics" of some of these antecedents suggests that they might not be supportive of certain aspects of the (black) feminist project. Anna Julia Cooper, who Valerie Smith correctly identifies as an important antecedent for contemporary black feminists, rejected any notion of a separate woman's curriculum and demanded that the gentleman's course, which is now popularly referred to in the academy as the European (dead) white male tradition, be made available to all female college students. Furthermore, Cooper's discourse, in "The Higher Education of Women" and in "One Phase of American Literature," is laden with literary allusions from the very tradition that many feminists would rather do without. However, since Cooper deals explicitly with gender issues in "The Higher Education of Women" and implicity through her concern with representation in "One Phase of American Literature," Valerie Smith assures us that Cooper has chosen the proper political position: she *"is writing as a black woman."*

This imperative to write as a black woman, *whatever that means,* seems curiously out of place in an intellectual project whose aim, from all black feminist accounts examined so far, is to advance writing by and about black women beyond the narrow parameters of traditional (black) male authored literary scholarship. For what it implies is that black women who do not consider gender a primary preoccupation in their work somehow forfeit their identities as black women writing. This prompts me to ask: Does Anna Julia Cooper's work on Charlemagne disqualify her as a black woman writing? And what about her very scholarly work, written in French, which deals with slavery and the French revolution? Does she cease to be a black woman writing because she deals with race rather than gender? My point is that if the black feminist project is to become more than the mere commodification of the works of a few black women writers and critics for the now very active academic marketplace, literary critics and writers must be allowed the freedom to explore the critical and creative forms that best satisfy their intellectual curiosity, even at the risk of offending others' political and ideological sensitivities. Even Zora Neale Hurston, who black feminists have claimed as a literary foremother, realized that to fall into the groove of saying what is expected is to take the path of "least resistance and of least originality." The writer can then consider him or herself "brave" for saying what the "Champions" of a cause already know by heart, and what other people won't even bother to read because they've read it all before.[48]

In an essay entitled "Art and Such" Hurston uses the metaphor of the singing black poet to show how *repressive* the themes of oppression can be for black artists struggling to satisfy both their personal need to develop their talents and the demands of their critics to be politically and culturally relevant.

> Can the black poet sing a song to the morning? Upsprings the song to his lips but it is fought back. He says to himself, 'Ah this is a beautiful song inside me. I feel the morning star in my throat. I will sing of the star and the morning.' Then his background thrusts itself between his lips and the star and he mutters, 'Ought I not to be singing of our sorrows? That is what is expected of me and I shall be considered forgetful of our past and present. If I do not some will even call me a coward. The one subject for a Negro is the Race and its sufferings and so the song of the morning must be choked back. I will write of a lynching instead.' So the same old theme, the same old phrases get done again to the detriment of art. To him no Negro exists as an individual—he exists only as another tragic unit of the Race.[49]

Not surprisingly, there are other black women writers who share Hurston's concern that "the song of the morning" might be choked back in the interest of what is fashionable or convenient. In an interview with Claudia Tate, Audre Lorde restates the problematic in the context of her own efforts to assert herself in the black literary community as a black lesbian feminist writer. "Black writers, of whatever quality, who step outside the pale of what black writers are supposed to write about, or who black writers are supposed to be, are condemned to *silences* in black literary circles that are as total and as destructive as any imposed by racism. This is particularly true for black women writers who have refused to be delineated by male-establishment models of femininity, and who have dealt with their sexuality as an accepted part of their identity."[50] Yet despite this "destructive" tendency on the part of the black literary community which has itself been "oppressed by silence from the outside," Lorde cautions against acquiescing to any kind of unilateral definition of blackness or femininity. To do so is to silence "some of our most dynamic and creative talents, for all change and progress from within require the recognition of differences among ourselves."[51]

The irony of all these imposed limitations is that, to some extent, black feminist literary criticism has fallen prey to this same tendency to insist on a unilateral definition of what it means to be black and female and to treat the "Negro" as "another tragic unit of the Race," a feminized version whose sorrow song repeats the theme of female victimization and multiple oppression. Black feminist literary critics have fallen prey to the academic spotlight, so much so, that black women writers, upon whose work the critics' work necessarily depends, often pale beside their critics' illustrious presences. Hazel Carby's rhetorical "non-negotiable demand" for equality with her black male colleagues at the Afro-American Studies conference is a case in point. Carby stole the show when she described what she called the "contemporary scenerio" for black women in Afro-American Studies and demanded that black men recognize black women as intellectual equals rather than "intellectual wives," "concubines," and "domestics":

> Whether we are black female graduate students or black female colleagues, our domesticized role is to serve as handmaids, providing the reassuring kisses and hugs, caring for, polishing and ironing, and reproducing the insights of the great men of African-American Studies. . . .
>
> As black women who are feminists, our bodies are being positioned in these very specific domestic ways, while the significance of our critical presence is eliminated. We are not your intellectual wives; we are not your intellectual concubines; we are not your intellectual domestics to be divorced or dismissed at your will. If you treat one of us,

graduate student or colleague in this manner, you demean and insult all of us.[52]

As Carby continued to unleash her "fury" on her male colleagues, a member of her panel could be heard muttering: "Hazel needs a body-guard"; but no one questioned whether the scenerio Carby created actually exists anywhere outside of her own rhetoric. Are we to assume, as she obviously does, that black women graduate students and professors are so overwhelmed by their multiple oppression, so victimized, that they have *allowed* themselves to be reduced to serving as "handmaids" to black male intellectuals? If the cult of domesticity has so permeated Afro-American Studies, how are we to account for the impressive scholarly achievements of black women, especially during the past decade? Indeed, Carby's rhetoric woefully trivializes those accomplishments and portrays black women as nothing more than helpless sex objects who *silently* heed the whims of their powerful black masters. I know of no black woman writer or intellectual anywhere who would fit Hazel Carby's profile. This makes me wonder: On whose behalf is Carby really speaking? Does her demand for equality with her male colleagues imply that there already exists equality among black women in the academy, including black women graduate students?

I can think of at least one instance where black feminism was not able, in practice, to live up to its own ideal of equality among black women *within* the academy, not to mention the black women who will never enter its hallowed halls. This was during a black feminist seminar that was hosted in the Spring of 1990 by the Afro-American studies department of a major midwestern university. The purpose of the three day interdisciplinary seminar was to bring together black women scholars from across the country to discuss their own work and debate issues related to the black feminist project. Initially, it was proposed that the seminar be open only to the participants and other black women faculty on the campus. For reasons too complicated to explain here, this was eventually decided against, and a compromise was struck: there would be at least one public session, and the department's female graduate students would be permitted to attend the seminar, but they would not be allowed to participate. Neither would they be invited to sit at the conference table with their Big Sisters. Some of us protested that this arrangement violated the very basic principle of equality that is so important to black feminism and all notions of Sisterhood. Others argued that since the purpose of the seminar was to create an environment where black women professors would feel comfortable discussing issues concerning their personal and professional well-being, this was the best of possible solutions. Still others dismissed the whole thing by saying that graduate students have nothing to say in the first place. And so the graduate students sat on the couch and in the chairs at one end of the room and *silently* watched as we sat at our table at the other end and proceeded to discuss and debate, among other things, the importance of unsilencing black women's voices. Occasionally, the graduate students made our coffee; they prepared our tea. They also served us cheese, crackers, and fruit. And they did it all without uttering a single word. What Michelle Wallace predicted in "Variations on Negation" rang especially true in this instance: *"Inevitably, we silence others that we may speak at all."* [53] Moreover, this incident underscores the existence of a hierarchy among black academic women. Even within the academy, all black women simply are not considered equal.

Similarly, Hazel Carby's frequent use of the term *intellectual* in her speech underscores the fact that despite her good intentions, the equality she demands in no uncertain terms is in fact limited to the women who already occupy the upper echelons of black feminist hierarchies. Intellectuals, no matter what their race or gender, belong to a special collectivity—*the intelligentsia* (and in this country they rarely include graduate students in their ranks). They are either regarded by the people and/or regard themselves as members of the learned class and as spokespersons for universal values (in this case the universal intersection of the variables of race, class, and gender). The implication of such "subjective" self-identification with the "universal" and with the collective subject, the intelligentsia, is that the intellectual must analyze situations in terms of his or her own universality and, in a moral gesture, prescribe what ought to be done so that the collective subject can enhance itself.

Michel Foucault has reminded us that the writer was once considered the intellectual par excellence, a "free subject" whose only aspiration was to be "the bearer of universal values." However, as intellectual activity became more specialized, the writer was displaced by new kinds of intellectuals whom Foucault describes as *"competent instances* in the service of the State or Capital—technicians, magistrates, teachers."[54] It might be better to speak of these new intellectuals as experts—individuals with specific cultural, economic or administrative competencies and specific social responsibilities. At any rate, Foucault explains that as "each individual's specific activity began to serve as the basis for politicisation, the threshold of *writing*, as the sacralizing mark of the intellectual began to disappear." An increasingly "global process of politicisation of the intellectual" meant the end of the writer as intellectual par excellence and the emergence of the university and the academic as "privileged points of intersection" of the process itself.[55]

Today, academic experts have coveted the vanished function of the idealized subject, the intellectual, whose task it was to engage in thinking and writing as activities that constitutively call into question most accepted norms and criteria of judgment, taste, modes of representation, and so forth. These experts in the academy have a different role from that of the universal intellectual, namely, to not embody a universal subject or value but simply to be high achievers through measurable performance in their fields or specializations. This does not mean that the *desire* for identification with a universal subject is absent: Hazel Carby's radical questioning of the limitations and shortsightedness of the (black male) *experts* who have helped to constitute the fields of Afro-American Studies and Ethnic Studies was undoubtedly prompted as much by her desire to identify—and identify with—a black intelligentsia as by the demands of an increasingly competitive discipline for high (professional) visibility. But in the academy, performance (publications, service to the institution, public appearances) remains the highest value. Professional advancement, pay raises, tenure, and star-status all depend on this final mode of legitimation.

Unfortunately, however, academic performances are played to a very small audience. Outside of the "new intelligentsia" there is no public, perhaps not even a potential public. Few, if any, of the invited members of Madison's black community bothered to attend the conference on Afro-American Studies in the Twenty-First Century. They either felt that they were not sophisticated enough to appreciate the performances or that the discipline itself no longer responds to their needs. Even writers tend to stay away from such "star-studded" events for the simple reason that they claim a different set of responsibilities. One need only look at the interviews Claudia Tate conducted in 1983 with fourteen black women writers to see that the writer is engaged in an ongoing struggle to reassert her responsibility to *writing*. She is involved with asserting her right to write what she pleases whenever she pleases, often over the objections and reproaches of the academic experts—the critics, whom Nikki Giovanni insists engage in literary analysis because they need something to do and they need to valorize what they do when they do it. "They need to write a book as interesting as the one they're criticizing or the criticism is without validity. If they succeed, then the book they're writing about is only their subject; it is not in itself necessary. The critics could have written about anything. And, after all, they've got to have something to do."[56]

And so, with a limited public and not much else to do, we have no choice but to perform for each other. And we do so while holding fast to the social myth that we are speaking for the absent and unrepresented *Other*. In the next chapter, I reflect on how that social myth has contributed to the current crisis in critical readings of twentieth-century black literature.

5 The Crisis in Black American Literary Criticism and the Postmodern Cures of Houston A. Baker, Jr., and Henry Louis Gates, Jr.

> Certainly one way to conceive of the Afro-American's attempt to resolve double-consciousness is as a struggle to be initiated into the larger American society. Such a struggle does not necessarily conclude in acceptance by that society. . . . In other words, Afro-American double-consciousness is not always resolved.
>
> —Michael Awkward, *Inspiriting Influences*

This epigram serves to remind us once again that Du Bois's "double consciousness," like the social myth that literary criticism can somehow speak for the absent and unrepresented other, is an abiding issue in Afro-American and black diaspora literature and literary criticism. And it is infused with the spirit of paradox. We can think of paradox as a rhetorical trope or as an inescapable logical principle of any system of thought. In either case, what we would find is that paradoxes are "profoundly self-critical." Rosalie Colie, who is perhaps the preeminent scholar of paradoxes, identifies three kinds of paradox: the rhetorical, the logical, and the epistemological. Each of these paradoxes carries out a critical function. They operate at the "limits of discourse" and redirect "thoughtful attention to the faulty or limited structures of thought" by commenting on their own method and technique. As Colie puts it, "paradoxes play back and forth across terminal and categorial boundaries— that is, they play with human understanding."[1]

In this chapter, I discuss how the current crisis in the critical reading of twentieth-century Afro-American writing has been deepened by certain philosophical and epistemological paradoxes arising from the incompleteness and inconsistencies of formal networks of principles such as the ones posited by Houston Baker in *Blues, Ideology, and Afro-American Literature: A Vernacular Theory*[2] and Henry Louis Gates, Jr., in *The Signifying Monkey*. But first, since I contend that this is a crisis in reading, I must also contend that I know how to *read*. Thus it becomes necessary to digress and briefly remark on the practice of the critical reading of literary texts.

Before the decline in the late 1930s of what Wlad Godzich calls the great age of literary history, reading was thought to be a simple horizontal process. The reader followed a line of writing or text in order to lay out its set and finite meanings and experience its truth. The critic, who occupied only two spaces in the academy—philology or literary history—was charged with securing the reader in the proper interpretation, and with establishing the texts and making them as reliable as possible so that they could be weaved into a "satisfactory narrative of national cultural achievement."[3] Later, literary criticism, under the influence of formalism and its interrogation of the meaning and truth of poetic analysis, began to turn its attention to reading as a problematic, as a complex relationship between the reader as decoder of signs, and the text.

Among the questions this new criticism raised was, in the "transaction" that occurs between reader and text, who has control of the reading of the text? The reader, the critic, or the text itself?[4] Where are the meaning and the truth of the text lodged? Do they come out of the text, or are they brought to bear upon the text by the act of reading? In order to respond to these and other questions, criticism became divided into the "complementary opposition of primary text and secondary discourse." According to Godzich, what this opposition suggests is that the truth of the primary text, which "remains somehow burdened by its mode of representation," can be attained and "given a better representation" by the secondary work. "In other words, the primary vs. secondary opposition is predicated upon a prior opposition, which it locates in the primary text, between a truth or a meaning to be disclosed and the means of that disclosure."[5]

In many respects, Houston Baker's *Blues, Ideology, and Afro-American Literature* is symptomatic of this opposition. Baker wishes, among other things, to resolve the oppositions between the truth of what he calls "Afro-American expressive culture" and its modes of representation. To do so, he posits a spatial metaphor—the blues matrix—that does indeed "summon an image of the black blues singer at the railway junction lustily transforming experiences of a durative (unceasingly oppressive) landscape into the energies of rhythmic song" (7). This spatial metaphor also summons an image of the folk, the blues people who, in Baker's paradigm, "constitute the vernacular in the United States," cleaning the dirt and grime from their always already overworked bodies, exchanging their old work clothes for their very best clothes and heading for the function at the junction. Here, the field and foundry workers, the laborers and loggers, the garbage men and the yard men, the cooks and the cleaning women and the washerwomen and the just plain wild women temporarily suspend their worries and their fatigue. And with the "dance-beat elegance" intrinsic to a "dance-beat-oriented people," they sing and they shout and they shimmy and they swing and they boogie and they otherwise stomp their blues away.[6]

It is in this space that Baker hopes to find and develop a methodology that will allow him to disclose a "uniquely Afro-American discourse" from which the Afro-American "expressive work" emerges. Baker argues that "the blues . . . comprise a mediational site where familiar antinomies are resolved (or dissolved) in the office of adequate cultural understanding" (6). His text is structured around a "guiding presupposition . . . that Afro-American culture is a complex, reflexive enterprise which finds its proper figuration in blues considered as a matrix" (3). To restate the problematic, what Baker seeks through the blues matrix is a critique of American cultural values. He is also trying to find a new way of apprehending Afro-American expressive culture that would adhere to principles of understanding and history that somehow stand outside traditional American theoretical contexts.

Henry Louis Gates is likewise guided by a desire to identify and define a theory of criticism specific to the Afro-American tradition from *within* that tradition. In fact, he claims that his work in *The Signifying Monkey* tries to accomplish, through the Afro-American notion of "signifyin(g)," what he feels Baker accomplishes with the blues in *Blues, Ideology, and Afro-American Literature,* namely, the identification and isolation of an "authentic" Afro-American literary tradition grounded in the black vernacular. Paradoxically, however, as I will show, the methods employed by Baker and Gates make the very notion of such authenticity suspect, to say the least. For they both appropriate and marshal formidable epistemologies from structuralism, post-structuralism, and deconstruction in order to make certain truth claims on behalf of the tradition.

Let me state at the outset that I do not find these appropriations problematic with regard to the explanation and interpretation of Afro-American literature: our positions in the academy compel us to "master the master's tongue"; our positions as critics of Afro-American literature should compel us to rigorously interrogate the "complex relation between [Afro-American] literature and literary theory."[7] Neither am I concerned with passing judgments on Baker's and Gates's degree of commitment to the study of Afro-American literature or to the black community, although I believe that commitment is an issue about which those of us who are black and within the academy must do some serious thinking. What is at issue here is whether Baker and Gates, in the interest of the black vernacular, have not in fact subverted their own intentions. This leads me to raise the very questions posed by Gates in "Authority, (White) Power and the (Black) Critic." Specifically, "can we derive a valid, *integral* 'black' text of criticism or ideology from borrowed or appropriated forms? That is, can an authentic black text emerge in the forms of language inherited from the master's class, whether that be, for instance, the realistic novel or post-structuralist theory?"[8] In an attempt to respond to these questions, let us turn first to what I shall call the two master concepts—archeology and ideology—of Houston Baker's *Blues, Ideology, and Afro-American Literature* and then to the coin of hermeneutics and rhetoric, which I feel governs Gates's rhetorical strategies in *The Signifying Monkey*.

In the first chapter of *Blues, Ideology, and Afro-American Literature*, Baker borrows his two master concepts, archaeology and ideology, in order to try to develop what he calls "Figurations for a New American Literary History." He uses these concepts in an effort to shift Afro-American literary study "from a 'traditional' to an economic perspective, from a humanistic to an ideologically—oriented frame of reference" (26). He relies on texts by Michel Foucault (the archaeology master-text) and Fredric Jameson and Hayden White (the ideology master-text) to effect this shift. Consequently, his discourse, indeed, his entire theoretical enterprise, is subtended by the spate of philosophical subtexts that prompt those of Foucault, Jameson, and White: the writings of Descartes, Nietzsche, Mallarmé, Heidegger, Hegel, Marx, Althusser, and Kenneth Burke, to name but a few. In any event, Baker's enterprise suggests a deep dissatisfaction—if not a crisis—with the way the fields of American and Afro-American literary history have been previously approached. But what, I ask, if anything, has been resolved in the crisis in the study of black writing by Baker's new technical elaboration of Eurocentric methods, concepts, paradigms, and so on? Does not his eclectic discursivity succeed only in more fully obscuring rather than revealing those modes of expression—the blues, for example, that are most firmly grounded in the black vernacular? I shall begin my interrogation by first taking up Baker's master concept, archaeology.

In his appropriation of *The Archaeology of Knowledge* Baker tends to reduce the text to a methodology, to a "method of analysis," in order to "discover certain primary linguistic functions" that he feels serve as governing statements for the discursive family of "American History." These statements, which include "religious man," "wilderness," "migratory errand," and the "New Jerusalem" are, according to Baker, the "primary conceptual structures" for the establishment of what he calls the "explicit boundaries" of "ethnic exclusion" in "traditional American literary history." He mentions Robert Spiller's *A Literary History of the United States* and an anthology, *American Literature,* edited by Cleanth Brooks, R. W. B. Lewis, and Robert Penn Warren in order to demonstrate his point that writing by people who do not fall within the category of the "Religious man," whom Baker describes as a "devout believer in God for whom matters of economics and wealth are minimal considerations" (19), constitutes a "category of the excluded" that exists "somewhere between secondary and non-literature" (21). In the first chapter, Baker aims to effect a movement from these "American historical statements" to a new structure. This new structure is governed by a statement, "commercial deportation," which he borrows from George Lamming's *Season of Adventure.* Baker feels that this "new governing statement" is capable of altering "the construction of traditional American historical discourse" since it signifies the involuntary transport, for profit, of human beings, "black gold" rather than courageous Pilgrims heading for "bleak and barren beginnings on New World shores yet to be civilized" (24). (While I do not intend to take it up here, it should be noted that Baker realizes that the *statement* also presents a fundamental problem for the archaeologist who undertakes to appropriate Foucault's archaeology of knowledge in English translation.) What Baker wishes to illustrate is that the "graphics" accompanying traditional American historical formations are derived from the category of statements that constitute the "New Jerusalem," whereas those accompanying the commercial deportation initiated by "an act of bizarre Western logic" are "strikingly different." Consequently, this new governing structure effects a shift in the larger historical view from a "New Jerusalem" to "Armageddon." Moreover, it "opens the way for a corollary shift in perspective on 'American literary history.' What comes starkly to the foreground are the conditions of a uniquely Afro-American historical and literary discourse" (24–25). In this way, the "archaeologist" Houston Baker feels that he has gone to a deeper level of discourse and has discovered certain formative principles—the economics and practice of slavery, for example—that subtend the explicit levels of American historical discourse. What is ironic, however, is that Baker can only discover European man engaged in commercial deportation through yet another "act of bizarre Western logic": through a massive importation of the theoretical and ideological constructs of European man.

This "act of bizarre Western logic" also clearly suggests that Baker sees Foucault's theoretical provocations as programmatic, although Foucault is not interested in constructing a method. While both Foucault and Baker are deeply concerned with knowledge of and the nature of historical change and with language as event or act, Foucault is perhaps more deeply concerned with the will to knowledge as such, that is, the "distinction between knowledge and the rules necessary to its acquisition; the difference between the will to knowledge and the will to truth; [and] the position of the subject and subjects in relation to this will."[9] Moreover, Foucault is acutely aware of the problems generated in the study of the theoretical problems themselves; for—and this is something that Baker seems not to have taken into consideration—problems are often generated by the very concepts one employs.

In the "History of Systems of Thought," Foucault writes that the series of individual analyses he initiated in a 1970–71 course was intended to gradually form a "morphology of the will to knowledge" from within the "history of systems of thought" (*Language* 199). His objective was to explore this theme "in relation to specific historical investigations and in its own right *in terms of its theoretical implications* (*Language* 199, emphasis added). This latter objective necessitated the construction and definition of the tools that permit the analysis of the will to knowledge "according to the needs and possibilities that arise from a series of concrete studies" (*Language* 201). Furthermore, Foucault always starts his analysis from within a unified "field"—political economy for instance—and he goes to great lengths in order not to remain trapped within the codes of such a unity. But more important, Foucault renounces systematic discourse and most certainly "structuralist ways." Following Nietzsche (who writes, "I mistrust all systematizers and I avoid them. The will to a system is a lack of integrity"),[10] Foucault in *The Archaeology of Knowledge* conceives of discourse as an "order" that, in his rejection of structuralism, he would like to subvert.

Baker does not ignore Foucault's disagreement with the "structuralist project." Yet, as he explains in a footnote, he brings Foucault together with Roland Barthes because he feels that in the conclusion to *The Archaeology of Knowledge* Foucault concedes "certain analytical successes" to structuralism (208n13). He also believes that Barthes, by focusing on the formation of historical discourse in his essay, "Historical Discourse," shares Foucault's concern with the "constraints of discourse" rather than with a "constraining subjectivity" (22). However, what Baker apparently overlooks in his reading of Barthes's essay, particularly in the third section, is the Nietzschean subtext shared by both the "semiotician" and the "archaeologist." Foucault makes explicit the extent to which his work is informed by that of Nietzsche in "Nietzsche, Genealogy, History." This has important implications for Baker's "archaeological" project because, in many respects, Foucault's concept of history mimes Nietzsche's genealogy. It therefore seeks to do away with the *theme* of anthropocentricism and the kinds of categories of cultural totalities that are essential to Baker's project. As Foucault explains in the introduction to *The Archaeology of Knowledge,* all of his work has been organized around an enterprise that seeks, as one of its objectives, to throw off the "anthropological constraints" he feels have prevented a close analysis of the methodological problems specific to the "field of history" in general. In return, he hopes to reveal how those constraints came about in the first place.[11] This enterprise therefore requires that history be mastered so that it can be turned to genealogical, or what Foucault refers to as "anti-Platonic purposes."

Foucault describes this historical sense as giving rise to three uses that oppose and correspond to the three Platonic modalities of history: the parodic, the dissociative, and the sacrificial. He writes that together "they imply a use of history that severs its connection to memory, its metaphysical and anthropological model, and constructs a counter-memory— a transformation of history into a totally different form of time" (160). Baker, on the other hand, is writing in the interest of "righting" American history and literary history, as we have seen (200). He also relies very heavily on anthropology. In fact, as he explains in chapter 2, he strongly favors the kind of "cultural-anthropological approach" to the study of Afro-American expressive culture taken by writers like Stephen Henderson and the Black Aestheticians (109). What he does not sufficiently discuss, however, are the limitations of his appropriated model for his own archaeological and anthropological enterprise.

Because Baker goes to great lengths to establish himself as a theorist— he even demotes Henry Louis Gates and Robert Stepto to the status of critics—certain sections of chapter 2 seem strangely out of place in his study (107). This can perhaps be attributed to the fact that the chapter is a revised version of an essay published in 1981 (64). What I find rather ironic about this chapter is that Baker takes issue with some of the same problems raised by Joyce A. Joyce in that very unfortunate exchange between Joyce, Gates, and Baker, which was published in the 1986–87 edition of *New Literary History.* Specifically, Baker criticizes the "recon-structionists" for being hampered by what he calls "literary-critical pro-fessionalism," a result of which is the "sometimes uncritical imposition upon Afro-American expressive culture of theories and theoretical termi-nologies borrowed from prominent white scholars" (89). He argues quite persuasively that the adoption by the "emergent" reconstructionists of the professional assumptions and jargon of white academic literary critics do little to further a "vernacular-oriented mode of analysis." It seems that Baker has not considered the possibility that his criticism of the would-be-theorists Gates and Stepto could very well apply to himself. Baker has a penchant for uncritically stitching together concepts, methods, para-digms, and the like. Thus, what he says of the reconstructionists, that their early manifestations "reveal a vigorous, if quite often confused and confusing, engagement with establishment theoretical language," is tan-tamount to the pot calling the kettle black.

Baker's theorizing does, nevertheless, raise many important issues about Afro-American literature, criticism, and literary history that have not been previously addressed. Indeed, his readings in the third chapter of certain canonical Afro-American texts are nothing short of provoca-tive. But his often wholesale appropriation has not served the interests of a "black vernacular" theory. Stated simply, Baker's theoretical inten-tions are badly undermined by his own eclectic moves. Consequently, what he observes about Robert B. Stepto's "critical rhetoric" is even more applicable to his own: it "plays him abysmally false" (93). It is not my intention, however, to rectify Baker's appropriations of Eurocentric phi-losophemes or his critical observations about other critics and theorists of Afro-American literature. I wish to comment, rather, on the impera-tives—epistemological and ontological—that guide his theoretical shifts.

One of these imperatives has to do with Foucault's "alleged" decentering of the subject. Baker makes much of this, yet he is forced to inscribe these troublesome terms within quotation marks. For example, in an important footnote to the section called "Defining Blues," he writes,

> The description at this point is coextensive with the "decentering" of the subject mentioned at the outset of my introduction. What I wish to effect by noting a "subject" who is not *filled* is a displacement of the notion that knowledge, or "art," or "song," are manifestations of an ever more clearly defined individual consciousness of *Man*. In accord with Michel Foucault's explorations in his *Archaeology of Knowledge,* I want to claim that blues is like a discourse that comprises the "already said" of Afro-America. Blues' governing statements and sites are thus vastly more interesting in the process of cultural investigation than either a history of ideals or a history of individual, subjective consciousness vis-à-vis blues. (206n11)

It is worth noting here that Derrida, in "Structure, Sign, and Play,"[12] points to a problem that is relevant to Baker's discussion of the "decentering" of the subject, that is, the process by which a referred to "point of presence" or "fixed origin" neutralizes or reduces the structure itself. Derrida suggests that the "movement of any archaeology, like that of any eschatology," might be complicit in this reduction. That being the case, then,

> the whole history of the concept of structure . . . must be thought of as a series of substitutions of center for center, as a linked chain of determinations of the center. Successively, and in a regulated fashion, the center receives different forms or names. The history of metaphysics, like the history of the West, is the history of these metaphors and metonymies. Its matrix . . . is the determination of being as *presence* in all the senses of this word. (249)

We arrive, then, at Baker's spatial metaphor; we arrive, then, at the *blues* matrix, at the junction with its "substitutions of center for center," with the blues and the blues singer standing in for the "decentered subject," with the latter transforming and translating the former in a "lusty and ceaseless flux."

Through his spatial metaphors—intersection, juncture, and so forth, Baker points to the figure of the chiasm. One of the oldest rhetorical or grammatical devices, the chiasm shapes thought and allows it to both take discourse apart and bring together contradictory functions, to gather

them within an identity—at the point of contact of *chi, X,* of movement. (I shall have more to say about the chiasm in my discussion of
Gates.)

In *The Archaeology of Knowledge,* Foucault also employs spatial metaphors, but he does so in order to destroy the very notions of experience
that Baker needs in order to place the blues and the blues singer at the
juncture. For the blues singer is charged with interpreting the "experiencing of experience" and with mediating the "endless antinomies" generated by the juncture's "ever-changing scenes" (7). The metaphorics of
space—even of an "original" textual space—dominates Baker's notion of
understanding because he thinks it allows for "mediation," although he
does not explain how antinomies can be mediated. In this space there is,
at least for Baker's investigator, who "has to *be* there," a spectacle, a quiet
spectacle with a beginning and an end. And so the disruptive play of the
blues, I would like to suggest, is tamed in the interest of understanding
and adequate explanation and interpretation.

Houston Baker appropriates his other master concept, ideology, from the
ideological models of Fredric Jameson and Hayden White in an effort
to avoid what he calls a "vulgar Marxism, or an idealistically polemical
black nationalism." (Because certain limits must be drawn in any critical or theoretical undertaking, I will limit my discussion of the ideology
master-text to Jameson.) Baker writes that his concern is with a "form
of thought that grounds Afro-American discourse in concrete material
situations" in such a way that one can gain the "subtextual dimensions"
of that discourse which have yet to be effectively evaluated (25–26). However, in the process of trying to reach these "subtextual dimensions,"
Baker sidesteps a very complex problem: that of defining the status of the
term *ideology.* To further complicate matters, in order to construct his own
ideological model, Baker relies in part on Jameson's "The Symbolic Inference, or Kenneth Burke and Ideological Analysis," an essay that sparked a
lively debate between Jameson and Burke precisely over what Burke calls
Jameson's "over investment in the term 'ideology.'"[13]

Jameson is highly aware of the problematical nature of the ideological model, as Baker points out. In "The Symbolic Inference," Jameson
calls ideology "the sign for a problem yet to be solved, a mental operation which remains to be executed" (Jameson 510). Its "usefulness" is as
a "mediatory concept: that is, it is an imperative to re-invent a relation-

ship between the linguistic or aesthetic or conceptual fact in question and its social ground" (Jameson 510). However, in describing his ideological analysis, which he claims to do phenomenologically, Jameson is careful not to argue for the priority of historical, social, or political reality over the literary artifacts themselves (Jameson 511). In fact, in another important essay, "Marxism and Historicism," Jameson deals with ideology as one aspect of the larger problem of what he calls a "properly Marxist *hermeneutic:*" it is a problem in interpretation, which he "construes . . . as a rewriting operation."[14] What needs to be questioned is whether Jameson's alleged "over investment" in the term *ideology* and his privileging of the literary artifact over historical, social, or political reality is an attempt to avoid commitment and falling into a vulgar Marxism.

That question lies beyond the scope of this study, but I would like to point out that, contrary to critics like Joyce A. Joyce and Norman Harris,[15] who argue differently, Baker and Gates are as concerned with the historical, social, and political implications of Afro-American literature as they are with deepening its literary analyses. In fact, Baker interprets the literary texts included in his study within the conceptual framework of the capitalist "mode of production." His interpretations are therefore situated within the tropes of ideological and economic practice. The shortcoming, however, is that nowhere does he work out the specific modalities or relationships of this practice. He simply asserts what this shift from a traditional to an economic perspective is expected to signify, that is, a social system "that determined what, how, and for whom goods were produced to satisfy human wants. As a function of the European slave trade, the economy of the Old South was an exploitative mode of production embodied in the plantation system and spirited by a myth of aristocratic patriarchalism" (27).

This sort of critical endeavor requires a meticulous textual laying out of the combinatory of the specific mode of production being interrogated and all of its "practices," for as Balibar shows in *Reading Capital,* the concept of "mode of production" is extremely problematic.[16] This, Baker does not do. Instead he proceeds by simply asserting that the negotiation of the economics of slavery should lead to "black expressive wholeness," that is, to the appearance of blues energized expressive *spaces* in Afro-American expressive culture that have heretofore been neglected by critics untrained in the "vernacular" (114–15).

According to Baker, Paul Laurence Dunbar's *The Sport of the Gods* is a case in point. Baker claims that the novel "gestures" toward what he calls "a blues book most excellent." But in order to develop his interpretive strategy, he turns first, not to a "blues-ideology," or a "blues aesthetic," but to an essay by Victor Turner entitled "Myth and Symbol." Baker feels that an interpretive strategy grounded in the kind of discourse employed by Turner will somehow help to "clarify the nature of Dunbar's blues achievement." He tries to justify his strategy by asserting that since literary criticism constitutes a historical domain, in order to achieve status as an accepted and learned critic, "one must transmit readily comprehensible messages to a historical (i.e., human, and defined implicitly as possessing determinate needs, habits, customs, etc.) audience" in "ordinary language" (115–16). What this has to do with Dunbar's blues achievements in *The Sport of the Gods* is anyone's guess, for if it clarifies anything, it is only that Baker is unable to remain within his own archaeological and ideological models. This also serves to inform on Baker's position vis-à-vis "critical professionalism," for his concern with the critic's accepted and learned status certainly contradicts an earlier statement that "The necessity, in all paradigmatic blues analyses, is to leave the 'bitter . . . rotten,' and, one might add, 'overly professional or careerist' parts alone" (111).

Baker does make an important observation about the status of the Afro-American critic, however. Being betwixt and between, "He is bound to engage terms of a traditional historical criticism in order to demonstrate its limitations. At the same time, he is free to move decisively beyond the inadequacies of a past historical criticism and engage Afro-American expressive texts in their full symbolic potency" (117).

Needless to say, such pronouncements have much to recommend them, but only when the critic is also aware of how such an engagement actually positions him (or her, as the case may be). In other words, the critic must take into consideration the extent to which the discourse he employs helps to determine that position and, as in this case, may in fact remove him from the very tradition he is trying to establish. For, let us not forget, *critique* is a European concept. Therefore, any discourse falling under the aegis of critique is already heavily informed by certain preeminent (philosophical and quasi-philosophical) texts from which subsequent critical discourses, including my own, cannot easily extricate themselves. This means that all of us are unquestionably implicated in the tradition of critique. The problems raised by this theoretical topography are obviously immense, particularly for the black critic, for what remains to be asked is, Where does the critic in fact "stand?" Whence and what has the black critic received? Where do those who receive his writing "stand?"

To properly treat these questions would require a painstaking account of the numerous mediations within this topography. Suffice it to say that as one who has "received" the writings of Baker and Gates, I am positioned in a way that compels me, in order to carry out this critique, to engage the very discourses being called into question. Stated differently, in order to adequately problematize the critical and theoretical projects undertaken by these critics, I must necessarily be traversed—*criss-crossed*—by their discourses. Theoretically, then, my "stand" makes me vulnerable to—or maybe it obliterates me from—the same kinds of criticisms I've made against them, for hasn't the pot once again called the kettle black? Perhaps. Or perhaps what is being demonstrated is how difficult it is for any critical or theoretical enterprise to support its claim against eurocentrism. Perhaps what is being suggested is that for a literary tradition that has been established by dint of exclusion, eurocentrism is the only ground.

I have indicated, albeit schematically, that Baker has in many and important ways misappropriated. The question remains, however, whether a more erudite appropriation of Foucault, Jameson, White, and all the other texts Baker grafts onto the blues matrix brings us any closer to specifying the black text. On this question I turn now to Henry Louis Gates, Jr.

Let us not forget that, like Baker, Gates is guided by a desire to identify and define a theory of criticism specific to the Afro-American literary tradition from *within* that very tradition. Before he can proceed, however, he must first clear the junction of the blues, the blues singer, and Houston Baker and place in their stead the figure of that sly simian himself. But, presumably in order to deepen the historical dimension of the Afro-American literary tradition, he must also invoke the Yoruba trickster figure, Esu-Elegbara, as the antecedent to the figure of the Signifying Monkey. As "points of conscious articulation of language traditions aware of themselves as traditions," these two figures presumably posit a "meta-discourse, a discourse about itself. . . . in the black tradition, in the vernacular, far away from . . . those who do not speak the language of tradition" (xx–xxi).

The language of tradition, of the black vernacular, is to be disclosed through an examination, which Gates carries out in part 1 of *The Signifying Monkey,* of how these two "tricksters" reflect on the formal uses of language in their respective traditions and how they "stand for certain principles of verbal expression." Esu is described as "a figure for the nature and function of interpretation" and for what Gates calls "double-voiced utterance." The Signifying Monkey serves as a kind of master trope "in which are encoded several other peculiarly black rhetorical tropes." By exploring the "place each accords forms of language use in the production of meaning," Gates hopes, among other things, to show the historical relationship between the two figures and the extent to which they "articulate the black tradition's theory of its literature" (xxi). A ritual of renaming, substitution, and analogue is therefore obviously underway as tradition becomes both a site of struggle and an opposition to the regulative ideas of hermeneutics.

In Gates's historical account of the development of writing by blacks in "New World African-informed cultures," Hermes is replaced by Esu-Elegbara as "the guardian of the crossroads, master of style and of stylus, the phallic god of generation and fecundity, master of that elusive, mystical barrier that separates the divine world from the profane . . . the ultimate copula, connecting truth with understanding, the sacred with the profane, text with interpretation" (6). Hermeneutics, which Gates defines as "the study of methodological principles of interpretation of a text," is renamed *Esu-tufunaalo,* the Yoruba term for "one who unravels the knots of Esu" (8–9). What he leaves out of his definition of hermeneutics, however, is the role that understanding plays in interpretation. For all interpretation must operate in the "fore-structure" of understanding. It must proceed from an understanding of the world and what it means to be-in-the-world since "any interpretation which is to contribute understanding must already have understood what is to be interpreted."[17] It seems that what Gates seeks to uncover through the genealogy of Esu and the Signifying Monkey outlined in chapter 1 is the possibility for this "most primordial kind of knowing."[18] Esu-Elegbara is inscribed onto this genealogy as "the indigenous black metaphor for the literary critic" whereas the Signifying Monkey is "he who dwells at the margins of discourse, ever punning, ever troping, ever embodying the ambiguities of language, [he] is our trope for repetition and revision, indeed our trope of chiasmus, repeating and reversing simultaneously as he does in one deft discursive act" (52). Gates is obviously playing off of—signifyin(g) on—Baker's spatial metaphor (and Derrida's *Margins of Philosophy*). Esu is at the crossroads, the Signifying Monkey is "our trope of chiasmus."

And so, we are at once forced to confront Gates's Eurocentrism, for it seems that the more the black theorist writes in the interest of blackness, the greater his Eurocentrism reveals itself to be. As Lewis Nkosi remarks in *Home and Exile,* "It is interesting that the further back the African artist goes in exploring his tradition, the nearer he gets to the European avant-garde."[19] Similarly, as Gates goes back in an effort to resurrect the myth of Esu as "the primal figure in a truly black hermeneutic tradition" (42), he must employ the research technologies of postmodernism and post-structuralism, so much so that, terminologically, they effectively replace both Esu and his "Afro-American relative, the Signifying Monkey" (44). In the process, both are de-Africanized, as it were, and in Gates's version, they "speak" like transmogrifications of all of the hermeneutical (Esu) and rhetorical (Signifying Monkey) paradigms post-structuralism has made ready-at-hand for him.

In some ways, Gates reminds one of his Yoruba-Nigerian friend, Wole Soyinka, particularly the Soyinka of *Myth, Literature and the African World.* Soyinka has made elaborate use of Nietzsche's notion of myth, and both Gates and Soyinka must have recourse to "mythic truth" in order to respond to the twin experiences of slavery and colonization and the cultural heritage left in their wake. In a sense, they both write in response to a critical, theoretical, and cultural hegemony, which they feel constrains African or Afro-American cultures. In a way, they also both seek to dislocate this hegemony by returning to—and supposedly arriving at—an "original" mythical locus that is inhabited by the gods, although Gates is aware that "origins are always occasions for speculation" (46). Both give priority to one god in the pantheon of Yoruba gods: Soyinka to Ogun, and Gates to Esu-Elegbara, who he places within the paradigms of origin and logos. "Esu's representations as the multiplicity of meaning, as the logos, and as what I shall call the Ogboni Supplement encapsulate his role for the critic" (36). The figure of the god of hermeneutics, which Gates uses to underwrite his interpretations, is indeed, in the final analysis, written over by a grave rhetoricity. In this way what is "manufactured" or "fictioned," is a theory of criticism that brings starkly to the fore the extent to which the black literary tradition participates in the one created by "white men." For as Gates is careful to point out, "Our writers used that impressive tradition to define themselves, both with and against their concept of received order. We must do the same, with or against the Western critical canon. To name our tradition is to rename each of its antecedents, no matter how pale they might seem. To rename is to revise, and to revise is to Signify" (xxiii).

But how is renaming revising? What is the reality of these (re)names in the Afro-American context? Can this kind of nominalism in fact yield a "black signifyin(g) difference?" Keeping these questions in mind, let us turn to Gates once again: "Lest this theory of criticism, however, be thought of as only black, let me admit that the implicit premise of this study is that all texts Signify upon other texts, in motivated and unmotivated ways" (xxiv). Here, Gates undermines his own efforts to establish a principle of black cultural identity based on a "black signifyin(g) difference;" and unwittingly, perhaps, he points to the traditional conflict within the tradition between "Sameness" and "Otherness." For as I have tried to show in previous chapters, to identify itself, the Same needs the Other. The Master needs to define himself against the Slave and vice versa. In cases where there is no Other it has to be invented, for a tradition is an order that requires mechanisms of inclusion and exclusion in the interest of the Same. Gate's notion of "difference," accordingly, is a notion of sameness. He therefore makes numerous gestures toward deconstruction only to end up in a kind of reconstruction.

For Gates, the Afro-American literary tradition is circumscribed by what he calls the "text of blackness," which he defines in terms of Ralph Ellison's notion of tradition: "a sharing of that 'concord of sensibilities' which the group *expresses*" (128). Gates is quick to point out, however, that this "shared sense of common experience" is not the primary factor in the sharing of the "text of blackness." He argues that the process of revision that tropes and topoi undergo when they are seized by writers as they read each other's texts is what grounds this "shared text of blackness" and the black writer in the tradition. For example, according to Gates, the Anglo-African tradition was inaugurated by John Marrant who used the text of Ukawsaw Gronniosaw as a model to be revised. Gates writes that his "idea of tradition, in part, turns upon this definition of texts read by an author and then Signified upon in some formal way, as an implicit commentary on grounding and on satisfactory modes of representation" (145).

These, then, are the grounds and the limits of the black literary tradition: to participate in the tradition one must read other authors in the tradition then signify on their works in some formal way, which would not be signifyin(g) at all. For as Gates so cogently argues in chapter 2 of *The Signifying Monkey,* an important aspect of signifyin(g) is its dreaded, yet playful "condition of ambiguity" (45). To signify is to engage in a spontaneous verbal game of one-up-manship that cannot be harnessed by writing. Consequently, to signify in "some formal way" is to deprive the game of that condition of ambiguity and the element of surprise intended to provoke a signifyin(g) response. Indeed, within Gates's critical paradigm, the disruptive play and subversiveness of the Signifying Monkey, like that of the blues in Baker, has been tamed, while the figures of the male and female slave and all they represent have been reduced to the figure of that lyin(g) monkey, and all in the interest of a "theory of the tradition." When this is considered in light of Gates's remarks in the introduction that the premise of his book is that "whatever is black about black American literature is to be found in this identifiable black Signifyin(g) difference," but that the implicit premise of the study is "that all texts Signify upon other texts, in motivated and unmotivated ways" (xxiv), one cannot help but wonder if Gates's "theory of the tradition" might more accurately be called the black tradition as Yale School rhetoricity!

As I stated earlier, Gates organizes and develops his theoretical enterprise around the practices of hermeneutics (Esu) and rhetoric (Signifying Monkey), with priority given to the latter as "the trope of literary revision itself" (44). Such a revision would therefore effectively mean that the tradition is beyond hermeneutics, for, let us not forget, all of the recent modalities of criticism that can be gathered under rhetoric eschew the hermeneutics of tradition. They see hermeneutics and rhetoric as antinomies. Thus, in spite of Gates, hermeneutics cannot be reduced to a methodology or somehow become a vehicle for myth-*emes*. It must, at least minimally, take up the problem of understanding's relationship to interpretation and try to grasp, in a given tradition, certain aspects of historical "consciousness." Textual aspects, therefore, participate in the cultural dimension known as heritage—or heritages—and are implicated in the Understanding. As I have previously suggested in my discussion of Baker's theoretical enterprise, ideological critique opposes this and finds alienation and distortion within the tradition. Similarly, a radical rhetoricity delights in pointing to discontinuity. Its operative mode is by definition deconstructive. This gives us an insight into why Gates is a reconstructionist in spite of his appropriation of the rhetorical mode of criticism.

This can all be more fully brought out by considering Gates's notion of chiasmus, which, as I showed earlier, is equated with the Signifying Monkey, "our trope of chiasmus" (52). I will have more to say on the figure of the simian after I have emphasized the centrality of the chiasmus in Gates's "theory of the tradition." Gates places his trope of chiasmus within a rhetorical field of "master tropes" which he claims have been identified by Vico, Burke, Nietzsche, de Man, and Bloom (52). He describes the chiasmus as the most commonly used rhetorical figure in black literature from the slave narratives onwards. It "is figured in the black vernacular tradition by tropes of the crossroads, that liminal space where Esu resides" (128). Since it is the "master-trope" of literary revision, we should not be surprised to find that the chiasmus structures Gates's critical and theoretical project itself: "My movement, then, is from hermeneutics to rhetoric and semantics, only to return to hermeneutics again" (44). The question that must be asked is how can one return to hermeneutics [the tradition] after rhetoric?

At the heart of the problem is Gates's metaphor of movement in the junction. His revision is a sort of Hegelian synthesis that yields the tradition, for in contrast to rhetoric, the chiasmus in philosophy is, strictly speaking, a form of thought. Thus, what I am suggesting is that Gates's use of the chiasmus is fundamentally Hegelian.

Since Gates has quite explicitly structured his critical context in part around the works of such prominent figures as Paul de Man, Derrida, and Bloom—in chapter 2 he superimposes his "figures of signification" on Bloom's "map of misprision" in a "signifyin(g) riff" (87),—I feel justified in invoking Rodolphe Gasché, a consummate reader of Derrida and de Man, in my discussion of the chiasmus. Gasché, in his introduction to Andrzei Warminski's *Readings in Interpretation,* offers a most learned and interesting treatment of the chiasmus as "a form of thought in which differences are installed, preserved, and overcome in one grounding unity of totality. It is in this sense that the chiasm can be viewed as the primitive matrix of dialectics in its Hegelian form" (Warminski, xviii). In this sense, then, the chiasmus is hardly a trope of rhetoric.

In bringing hermenutics and rhetoric together, Gates does not take into consideration the problem of the tension and actual discontinuity between the two. Rhetorical theory, in what is perhaps its most powerful articulation, that of de Man, operates within the concept of discontinuity between grammar and rhetoric. Gasché points out that in *Allegories of Reading,* de Man makes it clear that, for him, the chiasm is more than a rhetorical structure based on reversal or substitution. For him it is the textual structure of all texts. As such it cannot serve as a figure of closure as does the concept of tradition (Warminski, xviii). In de Man there is no possibility for a hermeneutical dimension that would be capable of restoring the truth of the text and its tradition. This would be to neutralize the chiasm, since it preserves no textual hermeneutical truth. As the structure of texts as texts, the chiasm promotes and prolongs its own rhetorical delusions. That is what makes it a text. So in this context, the issue is not, as Gates suggests, one of a reversal. The chiasm as figure is beyond reversal and revision. Hence the possibility of movement from something to something and back again is nullified. Movement itself is forever deferred (Warminski xviii–xix).

In Derrida, all writing is chiasmic, at least according to Gasché. Time and space do not allow me to go into detail, but I should like to point out that the chiasm as a writing practice has the quality of undecidability, since it is "neither simply constitutive nor simply disruptive of totality; rather, it is the figure by which a totality constitutes itself in such a manner that the reference to the reserve or the medium of dissociation inseparably in-scribed into the figure clearly marks the scope and limits of totality. No unity engendered chiasmically includes within itself the place of difference to which it must refer in order to constitute itself" (Warminski, xix). By definition, this conclusion would apply to the ensemble of *The Signifying Monkey*, which cannot itself be filled by that which it is trying to reverse.

It is not hard to see, therefore, that Gates is closer to the Master of dia-lectics, Hegel, than to the Masters of rhetorical disruption or the Masters of deferral and solicitation. But even if Gates were one of these Latter Day Masters, the following problems would remain: if rhetoric becomes literature or is literature's being, and if *as such* it is the phenomenon that, when analyzed specifically, would deconstruct the critical concept of the unity of tradition, then its *a priori* status would have to be demonstrated. To read rhetorically in the context presently under discussion means to effect such a deconstruction. Yet a principle of unity is essential to Gates's whole project, for without it the tradition would never start and Esu could not generate the Signifying Monkey. To some, this might be just as well, for there is a possibility that in the heritage of the Yoruba this par-ticular simian would be unacceptable. According to one Yoruba scholar, Oyekan Owomoyela, Obotunde means "monkey has returned." He also informs us that "[w]ith the exception of Edun (Colonos monkey), which the twin-loving Yoruba associate with twins, monkeys in general are re-garded with ridicule."[20] A more viable figure for Gates's project might have been the Signifying Slave or the Rebellious Slave, also of Yoruba ori-gin, for, "Once, there was a solitary being [Ogun], the primogenitor of god and man, attended only by this slave, Atunda. We do not know where Atunda came from—myth is always careless about detail—perhaps the original one molded him from earth to assist him with domestic chores. However, the slave rebelled. For reasons best known to himself he rolled a huge boulder onto the god as he tended his garden on a hillside, sent him hurtling into the abyss in a thousand and one fragments."[21] But this would mean the deconstruction of the Signifying Monkey and the reconstruction of the Signifyin(g) Slave and a thousand and one godheads. Of such stuff are heritages and traditions made.

While *Blues, Ideology, and Afro-American Literature* and *The Signifying Monkey* fall short of their emancipatory goal of freeing Afro-American literature from the hegemony of Eurocentric discourses, both studies bring into sharp relief what can best be described as a *nostalgia* for tradition. For to summon a tradition, for example, by reconstructing it, is to search for an authority, that of the tradition itself. Such an enterprise, even as it pits two or more traditions against each other, or even as it attempts to fuse traditions, is inherently conservative. Something is always conserved; something always remains the Same. This is what makes the role of the black critic or anyone else concerned with advancing certain emancipatory ideas particularly burdensome.

Blues, Ideology, and Afro-American Literature and *The Signifying Monkey* most certainly seek, through their theories of the black vernacular, to relieve the critic of his or her burden. But to try to do so by employing the methodologies and critical practices of that "Other" tradition is very, very risky business. For as Gates remarks in his analogy of Ralph Ellison's little man at Chehaw Station, "The 'little man' or *woman* is bound to surface when the literary critic begins to translate a signal concept from the black vernacular milieu into the discourse of critical theory" (65 emphasis added).

Toward
a Conclusion

As we have seen in the writings of Du Bois, Senghor, Césaire, Richard Wright, and Maya Angelou, indeed, in all of the contexts studied here, twentieth-century black literature and literary criticism returns again and again to the problem of double-consciousness and its attendant problem, *identity,* in all of its aspects. This preoccupation with identity, this desire for the reconciliation of the two "warring ideals" signified by the hyphenated name, by the *African-American,* by the *Négro-Africain(e),* is what marks much of the literature of the African diaspora as thoroughly modern. For let us not forget, in modernism the self is separated from its world, from its true home in the world. In modernism the self is homeless and only resides in writing. As such it participates in its own displacement even as it seeks to reconcile itself with the ordinary, familial, and social order of everyday life. For the "one dark body" of Du Bois's double-consciousness, that life has been doubly displaced, first by the Cartesian subject/object split, and then by the historical fact of slavery in all of its manifestations—in the social, political, aesthetic, philosophical, and so forth.

Let me state simply that in the premodern epoch, understanding was at once aesthetic, political, social, and religious, for it took place through the authentic procedures that allowed the self to be one with myth. There was an immediacy in premodern symbolic meanings. Meaning was at once subjective and objective. The self, the "I," was not isolated or distinguishable from the objective meaning of the world, the cosmos, and the social. Life could be lived as a symbolic re-enactment.

At the risk of oversimplifying, let me suggest, as Richard Wright does in "How Bigger Was Born," that modernism, as it makes its mark on black writing, is a kind of nostalgia for such possibilities. Which, if I am right, leads to these questions: Is there progress in modern black literature and art as Houston Baker contends in *Modernism and the Harlem Renaissance?* Is there progress in modernist literature and modernist art in general, or in the politics that governs them? Have our theorists—Senghor, Baker, Gates, Valerie Smith, Carole Boyce Davies—indeed, *have I* succeeded in loosening the double bind that threatens to impede that progress? Or have we, in our concern with elaborating a coherent theory of black writing, only succeeded in providing a basis for more theoretical incoherency? For as I have tried to point out in various ways during the course of this study, the theories that have been developed to address black literature also always try to contain it. Yet the writing continues to silently exceed all the theoretical matrices that try to address or grasp its being.

What remains to be asked, then, is what is the secret of black writing? Is it, as is perhaps the case with all literature—the secret of a kind of silence? Or what Toni Morrison calls those "Unspeakable Things Unspoken?" For when the writer is through writing the literary text, the poem, the work of art, she must remain silent *in* the work even if she chooses to comment *on* it later. For does not the end of the writing say that the writer has nothing more to say? At some point the writer ends in silence and the art work remains. Everything that could be said in the art work has been said. Is it this silence that justifies the critic, the one who must say something in spite of the fact that the art work has said all it can say?

Questions, surely, worthy of thought. For Senghor and Césaire, following the surrealists, for Richard Wright, following the existentialists, and for Maya Angelou, the black text, and black literature in general, like the modernist text and modernism in general, is embedded in paradox. It is a conjuring-weaving which reveals its dark shadow, the subtext of black existence and its un-said and un-sayable history, the dark shadow of one dark body, the one who *is* there but is never seen or seen to speak, the *shadow* of an indirect seeing, but persistently and insistently one who has always been and will be there.

Notes

Introduction

1. Joyce A. Joyce, "The Black Canon: Reconstructing Black American Literary Criticism," *New Literary History* 18 (1987): 335–44. See also Baker's and Gates's responses and Joyce's reply in the same issue, pp. 345–84.

2. Michael S. Harper and Robert B. Stepto, *Chant of Saints* (Urbana: University of Illinois Press, 1979).

3. Joyce, "The Black Canon," 340.

4. Norman Harris, "Who's Zoomin Who: The New Black Formalism," *Journal of the Midwest Modern Language Association* 20, no. 1 (1987): 37–45.

5. Ibid., 39.

6. Ibid., 41.

7. Addison Gayle, ed., *The Black Aesthetic* (New York: Anchor Books, 1971), xxii.

8. Jacques Derrida, *Of Grammatology,* (Baltimore: Johns Hopkins University Press, 1984), 158.

9. Harris writes that "the deep structural continuities [of the Afro-American historical experience] are well documented in a range of anthropological, linguistic, psychological, and historical texts by writers as diverse as Melville Herskovits, Geneva Smitherman, Alfred D. Pasteur, Ivory Toldson, and John Blassingame" ("Who's Zoomin Who," 39).

10. Anna Julia Cooper's "One Phase of American Literature was first published in her 1892 volume of essays entitled *A Voice from the South.* The volume was re-issued in 1988 as part of the *Schomburg Library of Nineteenth-Century Black Women Writers,* ed. Henry Louis Gates, Jr. (New York: Oxford University Press, 1988), 175–6. (All further references to this work are included in the text.)

According to *The Home Book of Quotations: Classical and Modern,* ed. Burton Stevenson (New York: Dodd, Mead, 1967), Sydney Smith asked this rhetorical question in his 1820 *Edinburgh Review* article of Adam Seybert's *Annals of the United States.* Adam Seybert (1773–1825) was a Philadelphian and well-published author who had a particular fascination for doing statistical annals. Cooper takes her question from the following excerpt of Smith's review: "In the four quarters of the globe who reads an American book? or goes to an American play? or looks at an American picture or statue? What does the world yet owe to American physicians or surgeons? What new substances have their chemists discovered? or what old ones have they analyzed? What new constellations have been discovered by the telescopes of Americans? What have they done in mathematics? Who drinks out of American glasses? or eats from American plates? or wears American coats or gowns? or sleeps in American blankets? Finally, under which of the old tyrannical governments of Europe is every sixth man a slave, whom his fellow-creatures may buy, and sell, and torture?" (I am grateful to Jackie Francis for tracking down this information for me.)

11. Paul de Man, *The Rhetoric of Romanticism* (New York: Columbia University Press, 1984), 126.

12. Immanuel Kant, *Critique of Judgment,* trans. J. H. Bernard (New York: Hafner Press, 1951), 150–51.

13. Cooper also includes the works of a number of black writers, including Frederick Douglass and Alexander Crummell in this "class."

14. Willam Dean Howells, *An Imperative Duty,* ed. Martha Banter (Bloomington: Indiana University Press, 1970).

15. Anna Julia Cooper died in 1964.

16. According to Herbert Aptheker, by 1890 Du Bois had already gained national attention, first as a speaker at Harvard's 1890 graduation ceremonies, and then as a speaker at the 1891 meeting of the "American Historical Association" where he presented a paper entitled "The Enforcement of the Slave-Trade Laws." *The Literary Legacy of W. E. B. Du Bois* (White Plains: Kraus International Publications, 1989), 2.

Chapter 1: *The Souls of Black Folk*

1. The impact of *The Souls of Black Folk* on the American public can be measured by the immediate reaction of the press. Herbert Aptheker summarizes the critical response to the first published edition in *The Literary Legacy of W. E. B. Du Bois.* The reviews are varied and go from praises of the literary merit of the work to suggestions that castration would be "splendid punishment" for "bad black men" who dare to preach about the "rights of men and brothers" and "golden gates" (41–86).

2. Robert B. Stepto, *From Behind the Veil,* 2d ed. (Urbana: University of Illinois Press, 1991), x. All further references to this work are included in the text.

3. In his typology of narratives, which includes Frederick Douglass's *Narrative of the Life of Frederick Douglass,* Booker T. Washington's *Up from Slavery,* and James Weldon Johnson's *The Autobiography of an Ex-Colored Man,* Stepto identifies four types of slave narratives. Each represents a stage in the development of an "authentic" Afro-American voice whose responsibility is to gain authorial control of the text's rhetorical strategies in order to tell the story—truthfully—of the

"pregeneric" myth of the quest for freedom and literacy and thereby validate the existence of the quester. The first is the "eclectic narrative" in which the voice of the former slave remembering his ordeal is joined by other "authenticating" voices that are not smoothly integrated into the text but appear in appended documents. The next is the "integrated narrative" in which all authenticating documents are "rendered by a loosely unified single text and voice." The third is the "generic narrative" which is discernible as history, fiction, essay or autobiography; and the last is the "authenticating narrative" whose "authenticating strategies" are its dominating and motivating features. *From Behind the Veil,* 3–5.

4. W. E. B. Du Bois, *The Souls of Black Folk,* (Greenwich, Conn: Fawcett Publications, 1961), v. All further references to this work are included in the text.

5. Martin Heidegger "Letter on Humanism," in *Philosophy in the Twentieth Century,* ed. William Barrett and Henry D. Aiken (New York: Random House, 1962), 274. (All further references to this work are included in the text as "Letter.")

6. Stepto writes that "DuBois's change of title from the original, more detached "Strivings of the Negro People," to the more personal and strident "Of Our Spiritual Strivings," in which the author's racial self-identification is not only more pronounced but also offered as a "given"—as something simply and profoundly understood by author and audience alike—is indicative of the new tone Du Bois sought while forging a book out of what he termed his earlier "fugitive essays" (*From Behind the Veil,* 53–54). Philosophically, however, what this change implies is that the particular—the social and political condition of blacks—is being reformulated into a philosophical or metaphysical problematic.

7. Arnold Rampersad discusses how Du Bois's training at Harvard influenced his thinking on philosophy and especially on aesthetics in his biography, *The Art and Imagination of W. E. B. Du Bois* (Cambridge: Harvard University Press, 1976), 19–47. See also Keith Byerman, "The Warring Ideals: The Dialectical Thought of W. E. B. Du Bois" Ph.D. diss. Princeton, 1978). Robert Gooding-Williams, in an unpublished paper entitled "Philosophy of History and Social Critique in *The Souls of Black Folk,*" has argued persuasively that Du Bois's involvement with the Philosophical Club and his easy access to Josiah Royce enormously affected his concept of history and helped him interpret it in terms of Hegel's *Phenomenology of Spirit.*

8. *The Collected Papers of W. E. B. Du Bois: Philosophy IV Notebook: William James: Lectures and Notes* (University of Massachusetts at Amherst), reel 87, frames 198–232.

9. Joel Williamson, "W. E. B. Du Bois as a Hegelian," in *What Was Freedom's Price?* ed. David G. Sansing (Jackson: University Press of Mississippi, 1978), 34.

10. W. E. B. Du Bois, *The Autobiography of W. E. B. Du Bois* (New York: International Publishers, 1968), 143.

11. John J. McDermott, ed., *The Writings of William James* (New York: Random House, 1967), 169–83. See also "The Notion of Consciousness," 184–94.

12. Bruce Kuklick, ed., *William James: Writings 1902–1910* (New York: The Library of America, 1987), 669.

13. Ibid., 671.

14. Frederick Hegel, *Phenomenology of Spirit,* trans. A. V. Miller (Oxford: Oxford University Press, 1977), 51. All further references to this work appear in the text.

15. This small but influential group of German intellectuals included Henry Brokmeyer, William Torry Harris, and Denton Snider. They were staunch abolitionists and willing to fight for what they believed in. Some of them even fought with the Union Army in the Civil War. They were also serious about philosophy. In 1866, they founded the St. Louis Philosophical Society. They also launched the *Journal of Speculative Philosophy.* From 1867 to 1893 this was the most important philosophical journal in America. Henry Pochmann deals with the importance of this group for the New England Transcendentalists in *New England Transcendentalism and St. Louis Hegelianism: Phases in the History of American Idealism,* (Philadelphia: Carl Schurz Memorial Foundation, 1948). See also William Goetzmann, ed., *The American Hegelians: An Intellectual Episode in the History of Western America* (New York: Knopf, 1973), and Stanley Vogel's *German Literary Influences on the American Transcendentalists* (New Haven: Yale University Press, 1955).

16. Matthew Arnold, "Culture and Anarchy," in *Prose of the Victorian Period* (Boston: Houghton Mifflin, 1958), 475.

17. Martin Heidegger, *Being and Time* (New York: Harper and Row, 1962), 194.

18. Ibid., 195.

19. For a very thorough reading of the Aristotlean notion of metaphor by analogy, see Andrzej Warminski's *Readings in Interpretation* (Minneapolis: University of Minnesota Press, 1987), xxxv–lxi.

20. Bernard W. Bell compares the Afro-American folk ideology with that of the German Idealist Johann Gottfried von Herder in *The Folk Roots of Contemporary Afro-American Poetry* (Detroit: Broadside Press, 1974).

21. Robert T. Clark, *Herder: His Life and Thought* (Berkeley: University of California Press, 1955), 260.

22. Herder perceives of the soul as a "composite whole, where all of man's powers and faculties work together in harmonious unity." See Joe Fugate, *The Psychological Basis of Herder's Aesthetics,* (Paris: Mouton, 1966), 10. And, according to Clark, Herder's concept of the *Volk* is derived from, and is illustrated by, the history of the Hebrew people. See Clark, *Herder: His Life and Thought,* 274.

23. Hegel describes the peasant class in the following passage: "the peasant class—the class of immediate trust and of crude concrete labor. Absolute trust is the basis and element of the state. In the developed state, however, the trust returns to one class, to the elementary point of departure and to the general element that remains in all, but which takes on its more conscious form. Thus the

peasant class is this unindividualized trust, having its individuality in the unconscious individual, the earth. Just as, in his mode of work, the peasant is not the
laborer of the abstract [i.e., industrial] form, but rather provides approximately
for most or all of his needs, so only in this inner life is his work connected to his
activity. The connection between his end and its actualization is the unconscious
aspect: nature, the seasons, and the trust that what he has put into the ground will
come up of itself. He tills the soil, sows, but it is God who makes things grow, the
activity being subterranean." Leo Rauch, *Hegel and the Human Spirit* (Detroit:
Wayne State University Press, 1983), 164.

24. Ibid., 164.

25. This desire for wholeness or plenitude is not unique to the nineteenth century or to the Black American, however. It goes at least as far back as the Middle
Ages when truth began to be thought as grounded in the certitude of the knowable rather than in faith. Before then, in the "pre-modern" Christian epoch, the
world was thought of as a carefully constructed system of intersignifications centered around an absolute and complete human reality. This was a "theocentric"
view of the world in which subject and object formed a totality: they were insepa-
rable. But when certitude replaced faith as the ground for truth, that totality was
ruptured and a new, anthropocentric view of the universe emerged along with the
notions of the self, the individual, and the subject which, in the Cartesian tradition, were split off from the world, but were always seeking reunification with its
other. What makes the problem of the relationship between the subject and the
object seem peculiar to the nineteenth century is the fact that it is the "domain"
of Hegelian philosophy.

26. Joel Williamson, "W. E. B. Du Bois as a Hegelian, 39.

27. *Parerga. Par* = around. *Erga* = work. *Parerga* = around the work. Kant
defines *parerga* as ornaments: "those things which do not belong to the complete
representation of the object internally as elements, but only externally as com-
plements," the frames of pictures, the draperies of statues, or the colonnades of
palaces, for example. It is not the primary subject. It is not central to the work of
art. Yet it is essential to it because it defines its boundaries. In so doing, it delimits
it as well. In *Verité en peinture,* Derrida develops his notion of the *parergon.* He
thinks of it as a frame (*cadre*), and shows how the *Critique of Judgment,* which
he treats as a "work of art" is enframed by the four perspectives from which the
judgment of taste is examined: the quality, the quantity, the relation of ends (or
telos), and the modality. Since Kant's discourse on the beautiful and on art rests
on his theory of the judgment of taste, it is likewise enframed—limited by the
parergon. Implicit in both Kant's and Derrida's formulations of the *parergon* is a
notion of marginality. In the case of the latter, what is suggested is that on the
margins of any discourse there are other philosophical or critical discourses which
"contain" it just as a frame "contains" a picture. The *cadre* is an "undecided" line,
simultaneously essential and not essential. The belonging together of critical dis-

courses presents a similar *cadre*. The epigraphs and bars from the Sorrow Songs that precede each of the fourteen chapters of *The Souls of Black Folk* can be considered the text's *parergon*. They are not central to the text but are nevertheless essential to it.

28. Lewis P. Simpson, James Olney, Jo Gulledge, eds., *The Southern Review and Modern Literature, 1935–1985* (Baton Rouge: Louisiana State University Press, 1988), 136.

Houston Baker makes these remarks during a panel discussion entitled "The Afro-American Writer and the South." (The other panelists were Daniel Littlefield, Henry Louis Gates, Jr., and Gloria Naylor. Baker's paper was published along with other selected papers in this volume edited by Simpson, et. al.) What Baker assumes is that somehow these "reproductions" of fragments of musical works and poems involve different processes of understanding and interpretation, an assumption that Gadamer argues against in *Truth and Method*: "I do not find convincing the objection that the reproduction of a musical work of art is interpretation in a different sense from, say, the process of understanding when reading a poem or looking at a painting. All reproduction is primarily interpretation and seeks, as such, to be correct. In this sense it, too, is 'understanding.'" Hans-Georg Gadamer, *Truth and Method* (New York: Crossroad, 1986), xix.

Furthermore, displacement and "deconstruction" are not coterminous, as Baker suggests here. Displacement, a term Derrida appropriates from Freud, is one of deconstruction's *movements*. In the introduction to his *Displacement: Derrida and After,* (Bloomington: Indiana University Press, 1983), Mark Krupnick writes that "although displacement is not theoretically articulated in Derrida's writing, it is central to his de-centering mode of critique. For Derridean deconstruction proceeds by way of displacement, first reversing the terms of a philosophical opposition, that is, reversing a hierarchy or structure of domination, and then displacing or dislodging the system. Derrida speaks of 'displacement' rather than 'revolution' because of his sense 'that the risk of metaphysical reappropriation is ineluctable,' and that this reappropriation 'happens very fast'" (1–2).

29. Derrida, *Of Grammatology*, 158.

30. These breaches and ruptures could be the result of over refinement by the early (primarily white) critics of Afro-American music who, unable to understand it, infused their own meanings into it. LeRoi Jones/Amiri Baraka takes up the problem of the "unintelligibility" of the early African-American music in "Art not Artifact," in *Blues People: Negro Music in White America* (New York: William Morrow, 1963), 11–31.

31. Henry Louis Gates, Jr., "What's Love Got to Do with It?" *New Literary History* 18 (1987): 355.

32. Onto-theology is a belief that what we call the real is present or can be brought to presence in discourse. In its onto-theologism, criticism claims to bring the "text" into correspondence with the "real"—with the world of meaning.

Chapter 2: Reading/Writing Négritude

1. Léopold Senghor, *Liberté 3: Négritude et civilisation de l'universel* (Paris: Editions du Seuil, 1977), 274. Further references to this work are included in the text. (Unless otherwise indicated, all translations are my own.)

2. I contend that in this context, Négritude as a discursive practice adheres to the same principles laid out by Michel Foucault in an essay entitled "History of Systems of Thought," which deals with discursive practices. See Michel Foucault, *Language, Counter-Memory, Practice* (Ithaca: Cornell University Press, 1977), 199–204.

3. Aderemi Bamikunle discusses the impact of the works of Frobenius, and interestingly, those of the Comte de Gobineau on Senghor's and, to a lesser extent, Césaire's aesthetics in "The Harlem Renaissance and Négritude Poetry: The Development of Black Written Literature" (Ph.D., diss., University of Wisconsin, 1982), 173–85. See also Marc-A. Christophe's essay, "Léopold Sedar Senghor as Racial Theorist: A Comparison of His Thoughts with Those of Frobenius and Gobineau," *Obsidian II: Black Literature in Review* 2, no. 3, (Winter 1987): 46–53; and S. Okechukwu Mezu, *The Poetry of Léopold Senghor* (London: Heinemann, 1973), 83–90.

4. Senghor's most recent biographer, Janet Vaillant deals with Senghor's participation in the French military and his incarceration in a German POW camp in *Black, French, and African* (Cambridge: Harvard University Press, 1990), 166–90.

5. "Cultural Soul" is the way Janet Vaillant translates *conscience païdeumatique*. See Vaillant, *Black, French and African*, 125.

6. See Michel Foucault, "The Subject and Power," *Critical Inquiry* (Summer 1982): 781.

7. Léo Frobenius, *Le Destin des civilisations,* trans. N. Guterman (Paris: Gallimard, 1940), 114.

8. In *Histoire de la civilisation africaine* (Paris: Gaillmard, 1936) Frobenius writes, "It is a question of the limitation of the faculty of human perception, which is, on the one hand, intellectual and conditioned by the senses, on the other, paideumatic . . . and conditioned by emotion. To this opposition between the most important organs we use in life, corresponds, perhaps, a split in the world that surrounds us into the domain of factual phenomena and the domain of real phenomena" (25).

9. The word "act" as it is used here does not mean "activity" or "process." Neither does it have to do with power of any kind. It refers to "intentional" relations between the ego, consciousness, and the self, and originates from the ego. As Emmanuel Levinas explains it in his discussion of Husserl, "Acts originate, so to speak, from the ego which lives in these acts. It is according to the mode in which it lives in these acts that one distinguishes the receptivity from the spontaneity of consciousness and from intentionality. The activity of the self when it is

attentive, in acts of creative judgment and synthesis, of assertion and negation, the spontaneity of the self in all its forms, must be faithfully described before being interpreted. In some of these 'positional' acts the self lives, not as passively present in them but as a center of radiation, 'as the first source of their production.' There is in these acts a sort of 'fiat' of the self." See Emmanuel Levinas, *The Theory of Intuition in Husserl's Phenomenology* (Evanston: Northwestern University Press, 1973), 50.

10. Ibid., 121.

11. Ibid., 45.

12. Jacqueline Leiner, "Entretien avec Aimé Césaire," in *Tropiques* (Paris: Editions Jean-Michel Place, 1978): 1, no. 1 (Avril 1941-Avril 1942): xix.

13. Foucault, "Preface to Trangression," in *Language, Counter-Memory, Practice* (Ithaca: Cornell University Press, 1977), 29–52.

14. Martin Heidegger, "Logos (Heraclitus, Fragment B 50)" in *Early Greek Thinking,* trans. David F. Krell and Frank A. Capuzzi (San Francisco: Harper and Row, 1984), 59–78. (I have relied on this translation of Heidegger's essay for my own translations of the italicized terms in the previous quote from Senghor's "La Négritude est accordée au XXème siècle" (*Liberté 3,* 234).

15. Heidegger, *Being and Time,* 51–63.

16. Senghor writes, "As an objective civilization, Négritude is an idea, I want to say a philosophy, and a life, a theory and a practice, an ethic and an art" (*Liberté 3,* 217).

17. Martin Heidegger, *Poetry, Language, Thought,* trans. Albert Hofstadter (New York: Harper & Row, 1971), xvii.

18. Martin Heidegger, "The Nature of Thinking," in *On the Way to Language* (New York: Harper and Row, 1971), 83. (All further references to this work are included in the text as *OWL.*)

19. Senghor, *Pour une lecture Négro-Africaine de Mallarmé* (Perigueux: Pierre Fanlac, 1981), 15.

20. Abiola Irele discusses the importance of intuition for Senghor's theory of Négritude in an insightful essay entitled "What Is Négritude?" in *The African Experience in Literature and Ideology* (Bloomington: Indiana University Press, 1990), 67–88.

21. Senghor, *Pour une lecture Négro-Africaine de Mallarmé,* 18.

22. Aimé Césaire, *Cadastre* (Paris: Editions du Seuil, 1961), 61.

23. Clayton Eshleman and Annette Smith, trans., *The Collected Poetry of Aimé Césaire* (Berkeley: University of California Press, 1983), 216–17. (I would like to remark that whereas Eshleman and Smith have translated the verb *déborder* as to transcend, I interpret it as exceed).

24. The very complex problem of the vicious circle principle is based, in part, on Bertrand Russell's paradox and his theory of types. See C. Chilhara, *Ontology and the Vicious Circle Principle,* (Ithaca: Cornell University Press, 1973).

25. Lilyan Kesteloot and B. Kotchy, *Aimé Césaire* (Paris: Présence Africaine, 1973), 235.

26. Réne Depestre, "Un débat autour des conditions d'une poésie nationale chez les peuples noirs," *Présence Africaine* no. 3 (Oct.–Nov. 1955): 36–38. (This article launched a rather long and spirited debate about poetry and nationalism to which both Césaire and Senghor responded.)

27. Ibid., 37.

28. Aimé Césaire, "Sur la poesie nationale," *Présence Africaine* no. 3 (Oct.–Nov. 1955): 39.

29. Ibid., 39.

30. Ibid., 40.

31. Ibid.

32. Ibid., 41.

33. Aimé Césaire, "Poésie et connaissance," in *Tropiques,* 2, no. 12 (Janvier 1945): 157–70. "It is not with his whole soul, it is with his whole being that the poet goes to the poem. What presides over the poem is not the most lucid intelligence or the most acute sensitivity, but the entire experience, all the women loved, all the desires felt, all the dreams dreamt, all the images received or grasped, the whole weight of the body, the whole weight of the mind. Everything lived. Everything possible. All around the poem that is going to be, the precious whirlwind: the me, the you, the world. And the most unusual mixings, all the past, all the future (the anticyclone edifies its plateaus, the amoeba loses its pseudopods, the vanished vegetation confronts itself). All the flux, all the rays. The body is no longer mute or blind. Everything has a right to life. Everything is summoned. Everything awaits. I say everything. The individual whole reshuffled by poetic inspiration. And in a more unsettling manner, the cosmic whole also" (162).

34. Césaire, "Sur la poésie nationale," 41.

35. Ibid.,

36. Leiner, "Entretien avec Aimé Césaire," vol. 1, xiv.

37. Ibid.

38. Césaire discusses in greater detail the radical potential of surrealist practice in "An Interview with Aimé Césaire," *Discourse on Colonialism* (New York: Monthly Review Press, 1972), 68.

39. Leiner, "Entretien avec Aimé Césaire," vol. 1, xi.

40. Heidegger, *Being and Time,* 212.

41. Ibid., 213.

42. Césaire, "Poésie et connaissance," 164.

43. Césaire, "Mot," *Cadastre,* 71. Eshleman and Smith, trans., *The Collected Poetry of Aimé Césaire,* 228–30.

44. Clayton Eshleman and Annette Smith, *Lost Body* (New York: George Braziller, 1983), xiii.

45. Eshleman and Smith, trans., *The Collected Poetry of Aimé Césaire,* 16.

46. Césaire, *Cadastre*, 77. Eshleman and Smith, *The Collected Poetry of Aimé Césaire*, 236–37.

47. Edward A. Jones, "Afro-French Writers of the 1930's and Creation of the *Négritude* School, *CLA Journal* 14, no. 1 (Sept. 1970): 18.

48. Leiner, "Entretien avec Aimé Césaire," vol. 1, viii.

49. A. James Arnold, "La Réception afro-américaine de Césaire: un dialogue difficile aux Etats-Unis," in *Césaire 70* (Paris: Editions Silex, 1984), 141–61.

50. Le I'ère Congrès international des écrivains et artistes noirs, *Présence Africaine* nos. 8–10 (Juin–Novembre 1956): 67.

51. Ibid., 68.

52. Aimé Césaire, "Culture et colonisation," *Présence Africaine* nos. 8–10 (Juin–Novembre 1956): 190.

53. Arnold, "La Réception afro-américaine de Césaire," 147.

54. *Présence Africaine* nos. 8–10 (Juin–Novembre 1956), 214.

55. James Baldwin, "Princes and Powers," in *Nobody Knows My Name* (New York: Dell Publishing, 1961), 27–28 (emphasis added).

56. W. E. B. Du Bois, "TO THE CONGRES DES ECRIVAINS ET ARTISTES NOIRS," *Présence Africaine* nos. 8–10 383. The full text of Du Bois cable is as follows:

> I am not present at your meeting today because the United States government will not grant me a passport for travel abroad. Any Negro-American who travels abroad today must either not discuss race conditions in the United States or say the sort of thing which our state Department wishes the world to believe. The government especially objects to me because I believe in peace with Communist states like the Soviet Union and their right to exist in security.
>
> Especially do I believe in socialism for Africa. The basic social history of the peoples of Africa is socialistic. They should build toward modern socialism as exemplified by the Soviet Union, Poland, Czechoslovakia and of China. It will be a fatal mistake if new Africa becomes the tool and cat's paw of the colonial powers and allows the vast power of the United States to mislead it into investment and exploitation of labor. I trust the black writers of the world will understand this and will set themselves to lead Africa toward the light and not backward toward a new colonialism where hand in hand with Britain, France and the United States, black capital enslaves black labor again.
>
> I greet you all and by the hand of my friend, Senator St-Lot of Haiti, wish you all good cheer.
>
> W. E .B. Du Bois
> New York
> 30 August, 1956

57. The six member American delegation included H. M. Bond, Mercer Cook, John A. Davis, W. Fontaine, J. Ivy, and Richard Wright. *Présence Africaine* nos. 8–10 (Juin–Novembre 1956): 407

58. Baldwin, *Nobody Knows My Name,* 28. Du Bois's outspokenness should have come as no surprise, for as Gerald Horne shows in his study of Du Bois during the Cold War era, Du Bois took every opportunity to fearlessly condemn American racism and imperialism despite the fact that he was, in subtle and not so subtle ways, consistently persecuted, often by friend and foe alike, for his outspokenness. See *Black and Red: W. E. B. Du Bois and the Afro-American Response to the Cold War 1944–1963* (Albany: State University of New York Press, 1986).

59. Ambroise Kom, *George Lamming et le destin des Caraibes* (Montreal: Didier, 1986), 35–37.

60. Baldwin, *Nobody Knows My Name,* 35.

61. Ibid.

62. *Présence Africaine* nos. 8–10 (Juin–Novembre 1956): 74.

63. Baldwin, *Nobody Knows My Name,* 37.

64. Ibid., 38.

65. Richard Wright, "Tradition and Industrialization," *Présence Africaine* nos. 8–10 (Juin–Novembre 1956): 349.

Chapter 3: The Auto-Text

1. Du Bois mentions the "omission" of "Freud and his co-workers in psychology" and the impact of Karl Marx on the "modern world" in "Fifty Years After," the preface to the 1953 Jubilee Edition of *The Souls of Black Folk.*

2. James Olney, "Autobiography and the Cultural Moment: A Thematic, Historical, and Bibliographical Introduction," in *Autobiography: Essays Theoretical and Critical,* ed. James Olney (Princeton: Princeton University Press, 1980), 13.

3. Marjorie Pryse and Hortense Spillers, eds., *Conjuring: Black Women, Fiction, and Literary Tradition* (Bloomington: Indiana University Press, 1985), 5.

4. Paul de Man, "Autobiography as De-facement," *The Rhetoric of Romanticism* (New York: Columbia University Press, 1984), 68 (emphasis added).

5. Ibid.

6. Ibid., 69.

7. See Addison Gayle's *Richard Wright: Ordeal of a Native Son* (New York: Anchor Press, 1980), 150.

8. Ibid., 151.

9. James Olney, "Some Versions of Memory/Some Versions of Bios: The Ontology of Autobiography," in *Autobiographies: Essays Theoretical and Critical,* ed. James Olney (Princeton: Princeton University Press, 1980), 236–67.

10. Claudia Tate, ed., *Black Women Writers at Work* (New York: Continuum, 1983), 4.

11. Ibid., 3.

12. Ibid., 6.

13. It should be noted that in her interview with Claudia Tate, Angelou admits that she was goaded into writing her autobiography *as literature* by Robert Loomis, an editor at Random House. See Tate, *Black Women Writers at Work*, 6–7.

14. Friedrich Nietzsche, *On the Geneology of Morals and Ecce Homo*, trans. Walter Kaufmann (New York: Vintage Books, 1969), 20.

15. Tate, *Black Women Writers at Work*, 9.

16. Jacques Lacan, *Ecrits* (New York: Norton, 1977), 58. With regard to desire, Lacan is speaking specifically about "man" as a human subject within the symbolic order. He writes, ". . . man's desire finds it's meaning in the desire of the other, not so much because the other holds the key to the object desired, as because the first object of desire is to be recognized by the other."

17. For a definition of the Imaginary and the Real see the "Translator's note" in Lacan, *Ecrits*, ix.

18. Jacques Lacan, *Feminine Sexuality*, ed. Juliet Mitchell and Jacqueline Rose (New York: Norton, 1985), 74. All further references to this work are included in the text as *FS*.

19. The Code probably dates from around 2100 B.C. when the Babylonian King Hammurabi is believed by some scholars to have reigned. The laws dealing with women, marital relations and crimes committed aginst women begin with number 108 and continue through number 214, although they are not arranged sequentially. The first of the fragments of the code was disinterred in December 1901 during an excavation commissioned by the French Government. See Chilperic Edwards, *The Hammurabi Code and the Sinaitic Legislation* (Port Washington, N.Y.: Kennikat Press, 1971), 42, 44, 45–51, 63, 99–104.

20. I think it should also be mentioned that, in developing his theory of the primal law, Lacan relies, in part, on *Totem and Taboo* in which Freud consistently refers to nonwestern men and women as savages or half-savages whose mental activity has not developed beyond that of children or neurotics. It is not my intention to hold Lacan accountable for Freud's racism, however, but rather to point to the pervasiveness of racist discourse in nineteenth- and early twentieth-century scholarly writing.

21. Hortense Spillers, " 'The Permanent Obliquity of an In(pha)llibly Straight': In the Time of the Daughters and the Fathers," in *Changing Our Own Words*, ed. Cheryl Wall (New Brunswick: Rutgers University Press, 1989), 127–49.

22. Ibid., 130.

23. Ibid., 129–30.

24. Ibid., 127.

25. In her conclusion to "The Permanent Obliquity," Spillers is willing to concede, "on the ground of pure (fictional?) speculation" that "the Freudian/Lacanian text of incest and phallic signification might apply to this [the Afro-American] community of texts—both fictional and historic—only by accident, which the writers sense more palpably than the sociologists." (148)

26. Ellie Ragland-Sullivan, "Seeking the Third Term" in *Feminism and Psychoanalysis,* ed. Richard Feldstein and Judith Roof (Ithaca: Cornell University Press, 1989), 43. (Further references to this work are included in the text.)

27. Henry Louis Gates, Jr., ed. *"Race," Writing, and Difference* (Chicago: University of Chicago Press, 1986). See especially Gates's introduction, "Writing 'Race' and the Difference it Makes" (1–20); Anthony Appiah's "The Uncompleted Argument: Du Bois and the Illusion of Race" (21–37); Tzvetan Todorov's "'Race,' Writing, and Culture" (370–80); and the critical responses of Houston Baker, Harold Fromm, Mary Louise Pratt, and Gates (301–409).

28. Gates, *"Race," Writing, and Difference,* 6.

29. Ibid.

30. Ibid., 402.

31. John Muller and William Richardson, *Lacan and Language* (New York: International Universities Press, 1985), 28.

32. Jacques Lacan, "The Mirror Stage as Formative of the Function of the *I* as Revealed in Psychoanalytic Experience," in *Ecrits* (Norton, 1977), 2.

33. Muller and Richardson, in *Lacan and Language,* caution against taking literally the notion that every infant must perceive itself in a physical mirror in order to discover its own ego. They feel that what Lacan is suggesting is that in the mirror stage a human form is the external image around which the infant discovers itself and the reality around it (30).

34. For a discussion of the "image" and Lacan's notion of the "complex," see Muller and Richardson, *Lacan and Language,* 30.

35. Juliette Mitchell, *Psychoanalysis and Feminism: Freud, Reich, Laing and Women* (New York: Vintage Books, 1975), 96–97.

36. The *Fort-da* game is based on the observations Freud made of how his grandson learned to deal with his mother's absences by playing a game in which he repeatedly threw a wooden spool tied to a thread over his crib while uttering *"Fort!* [Gone!]" Whenever he retrieved it he cried *"Da!* [Here!]." According to Freud, the game was related to the child's "great cultural achievement—the instinctual renunciation (that is, the renunciatin of instinctual satisfaction) which he had made in allowing his mother to go away without protesting." See Sigmund Freud, *Beyond the Pleasure Principle* (London: Hogarth Press, 1955), 14–15.

37. See Mitchell, *Psychoanalysis and Feminism,* 382–83.

38. It should be noted that in Lacan the child's utterance does not mark the mother's return, but rather the child's attempt to make the mother present in her absence. In other words, according to Muller and Richardson, Lacan sees this

game of disappearance and return as a paradigm of all speech, of "'a presence made of absence.'" See Muller and Richardson, *Lacan and Language*, 78–79.

39. Stephanie Demetrakopoulos, "The Metaphysics of Matrilinearism in Women's Autobiography," in *Women's Autobiography: Essays in Criticism*, ed. Estelle Jelinek (Bloomington: Indiana University Press, 1980), 180–205.

40. Mary Jane Lupton, "Singing the Black Mother: Maya Angelou and Autobiographical Continuity," *Black American Literature Forum* 24, no. 2 (Summer 1990): 265.

41. Janet Liebman Jacobs "Reassessing Mother Blame in Incest," *Signs* 15, no. 3 (1990): 502.

42. Ibid., 510.

43. Jacobs argues that in order for us to "understand fully the processes by which patriarchy is sustained," the child's "subjective experience of her mother as the most powerful figure in her emotional life" must be taken into account ("Reassessing Mother Blame in Incest," 514).

44. Françoise Lionnet, *Autobiographical Voices: Race, Gender, Self-Portraiture* (Ithaca: Cornell University Press, 1989), 148.

45. Ibid., 149.

46. Ibid., 148.

47. Heidegger, *On the Way to Language*, 134.

48. Ibid., 130.

49. Heidegger, *Being and Time*, 207.

50. Heidegger, *On the Way to Language*, 135.

51. Ibid., 133.

52. Lionnet, *Autobiographical Voices*, 149n.26 (emphasis added).

53. Maurice Blanchot, "Literature and the Right to Death," in *The Gaze of Orpheus* (Barrytown, N.Y.: Staton Hill, 1981), 43.

54. Jacques Derrida, *The Ear of the Other* (Lincoln: University of Nebraska Press, 1985), 35.

55. Lionnet, *Autobiographical Voices*, 151.

56. Sandra Gilbert and Susan Gubar, *The Madwoman in the Attic* (New Haven: Yale University Press, 1979), 122.

57. Ibid., 25.

58. Robert K. Merton, *Social Theory and Social Structure* (Glencoe, Ill.: Free Press, 1957), 302–4.

59. Gilbert and Gubar, *The Madwoman in the Attic*, 24.

60. Derrida, *The Ear of the Other*, 36.

61. Ibid., 16. Derrida, of course, is using this expression in the context of his discussion of Nietzsche's *Ecce Homo*. Nevertheless, it quite appropriately defines the two elements, Mr. Freeman's name and the image of the mother, that structure this part of Angelou's text.

62. Derrida, *The Ear of the Other*, 50.

63. Elaine Showalter, "A Criticism of Our Own: Autonomy and Assimilation in Afro-American and Feminist Literary Theory." *The Future of Literary Theory,* ed. Ralph Cohen (New York: Routledge, 1989), 347–69.

Chapter 4: Seeking the Other Women

1. Josephine Donovon, "Radical Feminist Criticism," in *Feminist Literary Criticism: Explorations in Theory* (Louisville: University of Kentucky Press, 1989), xiii.

2. Barbara Smith, "Toward a Black Feminist Criticism," *But Some of Us Are Brave,* ed. Gloria Hull (Old Westbury, N.Y.: Feminist Press, 1982), 157–75.

3. Cheryl A. Wall, ed., *Changing Our Own Words* (New Brunswick: Rutgers University Press, 1989), 2. All further references to this work are included in this text.

4. Carole Boyce Davies and Anne Adams Graves, eds., *Ngambika: Studies of Women in African Literature* (Trenton, N.J.: African World Press, 1986); Carole Boyce Davies and Elaine Savory Fido, eds., *Out of the Kumbla: Caribbean Women and Literature* (Trenton, N.J.: African World Press, 1990).

5. The complete title of Christian's essay is "But What Do We Think We're Doing Anyway: The State of Black Feminist Criticism(s) or My Version of a Little Bit of History," Cheryl Wall, ed., *Changing Our Own Words* (New Brunswick: Rutgers University Press, 1989), 58–74.

6. Elaine Showalter, "A Criticism of Our Own: Autonomy and Assimilation in Afro-American and Feminist Literary Theory," *The Future of Literary Theory,* ed. Ralph Cohen (Routledge: New York, 1989), 347–69.

7. Ibid., 347.

8. Ibid., 349.

9. Ibid., 348.

10. Gayatri Spivak, *In Other Worlds: Essays in Cultural Politics* (New York, N.Y.: Nethuen, 1987), 150.

11. Showalter, "A Criticism of Our Own," 348.

12. Davies and Graves, eds., *Ngambika,* 1. (All further references to this work are included in the text.)

13. Steve Paulson, "Scenes from the Afro-American Studies Conference," *Isthmus* 16 (May 3–9, 1991): 33–35.

14. Ibid., 33.

15. Filomina Chioma Steady, *The Black Woman Cross-Culturally* (Cambridge, Mass.: Schenkman Publishing, 1981), 7–48.

16. Davies mentions such inequities as lack of choice in motherhood and marriage, oppression of barren women, and the life-threatening practice of female genital mutilation (*Ngambika,* 9).

17. Steady's approach is perhaps even more sharply articulated in "African Feminism: A Worldwide Perspective" in *Women in Africa and the African Diaspora* (Washington, D. C.: Howard University Press, 1987). All further references to this work are included in the text as *WiA*.

18. This notion of complementary is based on pre-colonial African systems of belief that human beings are not fragmented subjects but rather "complete" persons within very complex social and communal organizations. John Mbiti deals extensively with the relation between the "complete person" and his or her community, kinship group, and "tribe" in *African Religions and Philosophy* (New York: Anchor Books, 1970), 32, 135–42.

19. I have previously outlined Boyce Davies's position on in a 1990 review of *Ngambika* in *Africa Today* 37, no. (1990): 71–72.

20. Carole Boyce Davies and Elaine Savory Fido, "Preface: Talking it Over: Women, Writing and Feminism," in *Out of the Kumbla: Caribbean Women and Literature* (Trenton, N.J.: African World Press, 1986), ix–x. (All further references to this work are included in the text.)

21. I have taken this term from Elizabeth Struthers Malbon's "Fallible Followers: Women and Men in the Gospel of Mark," *Semeia 28: The Bible and Feminist Hermeneutics* (Chico, Calif.: Scholars Press, 1983), 29–48.

22. According to the guidelines for consciousness-raising groups in *But Some of Us Are Brave,* one way that CR groups can act directly is by proselytizing, by "spread[ing] the word about the CR process through writing articles, and by giving workshops and talks" (53). My point here is that feminism, in some of its practices, is fundamentally religious. It requires the same kind of commitment required to be a good Christian or Jew or Muslim or Hindi or Voudun Priestess. Tia Cross, Freada Klein, Barbara Smith, and Beverly Smith, "Face-to-Face, Day to Day—Racism CR," in *But Some of Us Are Brave,* ed. Gloria Hull (Old Westbury, N.Y.: Feminist Press, 1982), 52–56.

23. Abena P. B. Busia, "Words Whispered Over Voids: A Context for Black Women's Rebellious Voices in the Novel of the African Diaspora," in *Studies in Black American Literature, Vol. III,* ed. Joe Weixlmann and Houston A. Baker, Jr. (Greenwood, Fla.: Penkevill Publishing, 1988), 1–41.

24. Ibid., 4.

25. Ibid., 5.

26. Chikwenye Okonjo Ogunyemi, "Womanism: The Dynamics of the Contemporary Black Female Novel in English," *Signs* 2, no. 1 (1985): 78.

27. Ibid., 72.

28. Ibid., 74–75.

29. Ibid., 75–76.

30. C. RoseGreen-Williams, "Re-writing the History of the Afro-Cuban Woman: Nancy Morejón's 'Mujer negra,' *Afro-Hispanic Review* 8, no. 3 (1989): 7–13.

31. Yvonne Captain-Hidalgo deals more deeply with Morejón's aesthetics in "The Poetics of the Quotidian in the Works of Nancy Morejón," *Callaloo* 10, no. 4 (Fall 1987): 596–604.

32. Alice Walker, *In Search of Our Mother' Gardens* (New York: Harcourt Brace Jovanovich, 1983), xi.

33. Maria Marcus, "The 'anti-feminism' of Hannah Arendt," *Hannah Arendt: Thinking, Judging, Freedom,* ed. Gisela T. Kaplan and Clive S. Kessler (Wellington, New Zealand: Unwin Hyman, 1989), 119.

34. Hannah Arendt, *The Origins of Totalitarianism* (New York: World Publishing, 1964), 159. All further references to this work are included in the text.

35. It should be noted that my view on this issue is purely subjective and is based on my personal experience on the academic job market in 1989. Although none of the job descriptions to which I responded mentioned feminism, during most of my interviews someone inevitably expressed "concern" that my work did not sufficiently deal with feminism or address gender issues. While I found this somewhat disconcerting, I was truly dismayed when a member of the faculty of the department of literature at a prestigious East Coast university called a colleague of mine to express her concern over what she perceived to be my indifference to black women writers *after* I had been offered a position as an assistant professor. My point is that feminism, in whatever guise it takes, must continually scrutinize itself in order to avoid practicing the kinds of repression it claims, in principle, to be trying to eradicate.

36. Giovanni borrows this expression about consistency as the "hobgoblin of little minds" from Emerson in order to comment about how inconsistency is a necessity for one's artistic development. Claudia Tate, ed., "Nikki Giovanni," *Black Women Writers at Work* (New York: Continuum, 1983), 73.

37. Edith Kurzweil and William Phillips, eds., *Partisan Review: The Changing Culture of the University* 63, no. 2 (1991): 218–19.

38. Aminatta Forna, "Kicking Ass," in *Conversations with Maya Angelou,* ed. Jeffrey M. Elliot (Jackson, Miss.: University Press of Mississippi, 1989), 162 (emphasis added).

39. Michel Foucault, "What is an Author?" in *The Foucault Reader,* ed. Paul Rabinow (New York: Pantheon Books, 1984), 112.

40. Cheryl Walker, "Feminist Literary Criticism and the Author," *Critical Inquiry* 16, no. 3 (1990): 551–71. (All further references to this work are included in the text.)

41. Valerie Smith, "Gender and Afro-Americanist Literary Theory and Criticism," in *Speaking of Gender,* ed. Elaine Showalter (New York: Routledge, 1989), 57.

42. Ibid., 57–8.

43. Ibid., 59.

44. Ibid.

45. Fortunately, most black feminists involved with literary studies insist on "good scholarship." But at least one white feminist feels that "good and careful scholarship" is secondary to the relationships that white women can establish with black women by working on black women's texts. In "Race and Gender in Feminist Theory," Carrie Jane Singleton writes, "I undertook this essay to question my own position as a white woman scholar. I think one direction in which white feminists should extend the analysis offered thus far is to questions of scholarship and the production of knowledge in our culture. Politically, what are the implications of white women producing knowledge about Black women? An argument that I have often heard in defense of white women's ability to work with Black women's texts is, 'If it is good and careful scholarship, it must be all right.' To make careful scholarship the only cirterion is to once again isolate the academy, and to ignore the historical construction of power relationships between Black and white women. Whether or not one does good or bad scholarship, I think, is secondary. The more fundamental question is, what does it mean to produce knowledge and in production, what relationships are created by the scholar?" *Sage: A Scholarly Journal on Black Women* 6, no. 1 (1989): 12–17.

46. Gayl Jones discusses Hurston's relation to feminism in an interview with Michael Harper. Interestingly, Jones remarks that while most feminists identify with Hurston's characterizations of strong black women, there are a number of things in her fiction that certain feminists would "have gotten on her about." For example, she feels that "the feminists" would probably not have liked the idea of the woman "serving" in *Seraph on the Suwanee*. See "Gayl Jones, an Interview," in *Chant of Saints,* ed. Michael Harper and Robert Stepto (Urbana: University of Illinois Press, 1979), 363.

47. Valerie Smith, "Gender and Afro-Americanist Literary Theory and Criticism," 62 (emphasis added).

48. Zora Neale Hurston, "Art and Such," in *Reading Black, Reading Feminist,* ed. Henry Louis Gates, Jr. (New York: Meridian, 1990), 24.

49. Ibid., 24.

50. Claudia Tate, *Black Women Writers at Work,* 101 (emphasis added).

51. Ibid., 101.

52. This speech, like the rest of the conference proceedings, were tape recorded. Some of the papers presented at the conference were revised and published in the *Black Scholar* 22, no. 3 (Summer 1992). This one was not. The transcription of Carby's speech is my own.

53. Michelle Wallace, "Variations on Negation and the Heresy of Black Feminist Creativity," *Reading Black, Reading Feminist,* ed. Henry Louis Gates, Jr. (New York, N.Y.: Meridian, 1990), 59, emphasis added.

54. Michel Foucault, "Truth and Power," *Power/Knowledge: Selected Interviews and Other Writings, 1972–1977,* ed. Colin Gordon (New York: Pantheon Books, 1980), 126.

55. Ibid., 127.

56. Claudia Tate, *Black Women Writers at Work,* 62–63.

Chapter 5: The Crisis in Black American Literary Criticism

A version of this essay first appeared in *Diacritics* (Winter 1990): 43–56. Reprinted with permission of the Journal.

1. Rosalie Colie, *Paradoxia Epidemica: The Renaissance Tradition of Paradox* (Princeton: Princeton University Press, 1966), 7.

2. Houston Baker, *Blues, Ideology, and Afro-American Literature* (All further references to this work are included in the text.)

3. Wlad Godzich, "Caution! Reader at Work!" in *Blindness and Insight,* ed. Paul de Man (Minneapolis: University of Minnesota Press, 1983), xvii.

4. This notion of reading as a *transaction* between a reader and a text was taken from Louise Rosenblatt's "On the Aesthetic as the Basic Model of the Reading Process," *Bucknell Review* 26, no. 1 (1981): 17–32.

5. Godzich, "Caution! Reader at Work!" xxiii.

6. Albert Murray, *Stomping the Blues* (New York: McGraw-Hill, 1976), 257.

7. Henry Louis Gates, Jr., "Authority, (White) Power and the (Black) Critic; It's All Greek to Me," *Cultural Critique* no. 7 (Fall 1987): 36.

8. Ibid.

9. Michel Foucault, *Language, Counter-Memory, Practice,* trans., Donald Bouchard (Ithaca: Cornell University Press, 1977), 201.

10. Frederich Nietzsche, "Twilight of the Idols," in *The Portable Nietzsche,* ed. Walter Kaufmann (New York: Penguin Books, 1968), 470.

11. Foucault, *The Archaeology of Knowledge* (New York: Harper and Row, 1972), 15.

12. Jacques Derrida, "Structure, Sign, and Play in the Discourse of the Human Sciences," in *The Languages of Criticism and the Sciences of Man,* ed. Richard Macksey and Eugenio Donato (Baltimore: Johns Hopkins Press, 1970), 247–72.

13. See Fredric Jameson, "The Symbolic Inference; or, Kenneth Burke and Ideological Analysis," *Critical Inquiry* 4 (1978): 507–22, and the Burke-Jameson critical responses in vol. 5, 401–22.

14. Jameson, "Marxism and Historicism," in *The Ideologies of Theory,* vol. 2 (Minneapolis: University of Minnesota Press, 1988), 148.

15. Norman Harris, "Who's Zoomin' Who": The New Black Formalism," *Journal of the Midwest Modern Language Association* 20, no. 1 (1987): 37–45. It should be noted that this essay does not mention Baker. It deals instead with Gates's and Robert Stepto's presumed lack of concern for the social and political in their critical practices.

16. Etienne Balibar, "On the Basic Concepts of Historical Materialism," in

Reading Capital (London: The Gresham Press, 1977), 201–308. See especially pp. 230–33, 247.

17. Heidegger, *Being and Time,* 194.

18. Ibid., 194.

19. Lewis Nkosi, *Home and Exile* (London: Longmans, 1965), 113.

20. Oyekan Owomoyela, "The Phantom of Nigerian Theater," *African Studies Review* 22, no. 1 (Apr. 1979): 43.

21. Wole Soyinka, *Myth, Literature and the African World* (Cambridge: Cambridge University Press, 1976), 27.

Selected Bibliography

Angelou, Maya. *I Know Why the Caged Bird Sings*. New York: Bantam Books, 1971.

Althusser, Louis, and Etienne Balibar. *Reading Capital*. London: Gresham Press, 1977.

Aptheker, Herbert. *The Literary Legacy of W. E. B. Du Bois*. White Plains: Kraus International Publications, 1989.

Arendt, Hannah. *The Origins of Totalitarianism*. New York: World Publishing, 1964.

Arnold, A. James. "La Réception afro-américaine: un dialogue difficile aux Etats-Unis." In *Césaire 70*. Ed. Ngal et Steins, 141–62. Paris: Editions Silex, 1984.

Awkward, Michael. *Inspiriting Influences*. New York: Columbia University Press, 1989.

Baker, Houston A., Jr. *Blues, Ideology, and Afro-American Literature: A Vernacular Theory*. Chicago: University of Chicago Press, 1984.

———. *Modernism and the Harlem Renaissance*. Chicago: University of Chicago Press, 1987.

Baldwin, James. *Nobody Knows My Name*. New York: Dell Publishing, 1960.

Bamikunle, Aderemi. "The Harlem Renaissance and Négritude Poetry: The Development of Black Written Literature." Ph.D. diss., University of Wisconsin-Madison, 1982.

Bell, Bernard. *The Folk Roots of Contemporary Afro-American Poetry*. Detroit: Broadside Press, 1974.

Blanchot, Maurice. *The Gaze of Orpheus*. Barrytown, N.Y.: Staton Hill, 1981.

Buckler, W. E., ed. *Prose of the Victorian Period*. Boston: Houghton Mifflin, 1958.

Byerman, Keith. "The Warring Ideals: The Dialectical Thought of W. E. B. Du Bois." Ph.D. diss., Princeton University, 1978.

Césaire, Aimé. "Sur la poésie nationale." *Présence Africaine* No. 3 (Oct.–Nov. 1955).

———. "Culture et colonisation." *Présence Africaine* Nos. 8–10, 1956.

———. *Cadastre*. Paris: Editions du Seuil, 1961.

———. *Discourse on Colonialism*. New York: Monthly Review Press, 1972.

———. "Poésie et connaissance." In *Tropiques*. Paris: Editions Jean-Michel Place, 1978.

Chihara, C. *Ontology and the Vicious Circle Principle*. Ithaca: Cornell University Press, 1973.

Christophe, Marc-A. "Léopold Sedar Senghor as Racial Theorist: A Comparison of His Thoughts with Those of Frobenius and Gobineau." *Obsidian II: Black Literature in Review* 2, no. 3 (Winter 1987): 46–53.

Clark, Robert T. *Herder: His Life and Thought.* Berkeley: University of California Press, 1955.

Cohen, Ralph, ed. *The Future of Literary Theory.* New York: Routledge, 1989.

Colie, Rosalie. *Paradoxia Epidemica.* Princeton: Princeton University Press, 1966.

Cooper, Anna J. *A Voice from the South.* New York: Oxford University Press, 1988.

Davies, Carole Boyce and Anne Adams Graves, eds. *Ngambika.* Trenton, N.J.: African World Press, 1986.

Davies, Carole Boyce and Elaine Savory Fido, eds. *Out of the Kumbla: Caribbean Women and Literature.* Trenton, N.J.: African World Press, 1990.

De Man, Paul. *Blindness and Insight.* Minneapolis: University of Minnesota Press, 1983.

———. *The Rhetoric of Romanticism.* New York: Columbia University Press, 1984.

Depestre, René. "Un débat autour des conditions d'une poésie nationale chez les peuples noirs." *Présence Africaine* No. 3 (Oct.–Nov. 1955): 36–38.

Derrida, Jacques. *La Vérite en peinture.* Paris: Flammarion, 1978.

———. *Of Grammatology.* Baltimore: Johns Hopkins University Press, 1984.

———. *The Ear of the Other.* Lincoln: University of Nebraska Press, 1985.

Donovon, Josephine. *Feminist Literary Criticism.* Louisville: University of Kentucky Press, 1989.

Du Bois, W. E. B. *The Souls of Black Folk.* New York: Fawcett Publications, 1964.

———. *The Autobiography of W. E. B. Du Bois.* New York: International Publishers, 1970.

———. *The Collected Papers of W. E. B. Du Bois: Philosophy IV Notebook: William James Lecture and Notes.* University of Massachusetts at Amherst. Reel 87, frames 198–232. Microfilm.

Edwards, Chilperic. *The Hammurabi Code and the Sinaitic Legislation.* Port Washington, N.Y.: Kennikat Press, 1971.

Elliot, Jeffrey M., ed. *Conversations with Maya Angelou.* Jackson Miss.: University Press of Mississippi, 1989.

Eshleman, Clayton, and Annette Smith, trans. *The Collected Poetry of Aimé Césaire.* Berkeley: University of California Press, 1983.

———. *Lost Body.* New York: Braziller, 1986.

Feldstein, Richard and Judith Roof, eds. *Feminism and Psychoanalysis.* Ithaca: Cornell University Press, 1989.

Foucault, Michel. *The Archaeology of Knowledge.* New York: Harper and Row, 1972.

———. *Language, Counter-Memory, Practice.* Ithaca: Cornell University Press, 1977.

———. *Power/Knowledge.* New York: Pantheon Books, 1977.

———. "The Subject and Power." *Critical Inquiry* (Summer 1982): 777–95.

Frobenius, Léo. *Histoire de la civilisation africaine.* Paris: Gaillmard, 1936.

———. *Le Destin des civilisations.* Paris: Gallimard, 1940.

Freud, Sigmund. *Beyond the Pleasure Principle.* London: Hogarth Press, 1955.

Fugate, Joe. *The Psychological Basis of Herder's Aesthetics.* Paris: Mouton and Co, 1966.

Gadamer, Hans-Georg. *Truth and Method.* New York: Crossroad, 1986.

Gates, Henry Louis, Jr. *Black Literature and Literary Theory.* New York: Methuen, 1984.

———. *"Race," Writing, and Difference.* Chicago: University of Chicago Press, 1986.

———. "Authority, (White) Power and the (Black Critic; Its All Greek to Me." *Cultural Critique* 7 (1987): 19–46.

———. *The Signifying Monkey.* Oxford: Oxford University Press, 1988.

———. *Reading Black, Reading Feminist.* New York: Meridian, 1990.

Gayle, Addison. *The Black Aesthetic.* New York: Anchor Books, 1971.

———. *Richard Wright: Ordeal of a Native Son.* New York: Anchor Press, 1980.

Gilbert, Sandra, and Susan Gubar. *The Madwoman in the Attic.* New Haven: Yale University Press, 1979.

Goetzmann, William, ed. *The American Hegelians: An Intellectual Episode in the History of Western America.* New York: Knopf, 1973.

Gooding-Williams, Robert. "Philosophy of History and Social Critique in *The Souls of Black Folk.*" (Paper).

Harari, J., ed. *Textual Strategies.* New York: Cornell University Press, 1979.

Harper, Michael, and Robert B. Stepto, eds. *Chant of Saints.* Urbana: University of Illinois Press, 1979.

Harris, Norman. "Who's Zoomin Who: The New Black Formalism." *Journal of the Midwest Modern Language Association* 20, no. 1 (1987): 37–45.

Hegel, Frederick. *Phenomenology of Spirit.* Trans. A. V. Miller. Oxford: Oxford University Press, 1952.

Heidegger, Martin. *Being and Time.* New York: Harper and Row, 1962.

———. "Letter on Humanism." In *Philosophy in the Twentieth Century.* Ed. William Barrett and Henry D. Aiken, 270–302. New York: Random House, 1962.

———. *On The Way to Language.* New York: Harper and Row, 1971.

———. *Poetry, Language, and Thought.* New York: Harper and Row, 1971.

———. *Early Greek Thinking.* New York: Harper and Row, 1984.

Hidalgo, Yvonne Capitain. "The Poetics of the Quotidian in the Works of Nancy Morejón." *Callaloo* 10, no. 4 (Fall 1987): 596–604.

Horne, Gerald. *Black and Red: W. E. B. Du Bois and the Afro-American Response to the Cold War 1944–1963.* Albany: State University of New York Press, 1986.

Howells, William Dean. *An Imperative Duty.* Bloomington: Indiana University Press, 1970.

Hull, Gloria, ed. *But Some of Us Are Brave*. Old Westbury, N.Y.: Feminist Press, 1982.

Irele, Abiola. *The African Experience in Literature and Ideology*. Bloomington: Indiana University Press, 1990.

Jacobs, Janet L. "Reassessing Mother Blame in Incest." *Signs* 15, no. 3 (1990): 500–514.

James, William. "Hegel and His Method." In *William James: Writings, 1902–1910*. Ed. Bruce Kuklick, 668–89. New York: Library of America, 1987.

Jameson, Fredric. "Ideology and Symbolic Action. *Critical Inquiry* 5 (1978): 417–422.

———. "The Symbolic Inference; or, Kenneth Burke and Ideological Analysis." *Critical Inquiry* 4 (1978): 417–22.

———. *The Ideologies of Theory, Vol. 2*. Minneapolis: University of Minnesota Press, 1988.

Jelinek, Estelle, ed. *Women's Autobiography: Essays in Criticism*. Bloomington: Indiana University Press, 1980.

Jones, Edward A. "Afro-French Writers of the 1930's and Creation of the *Négritude* School." *CLA Journal* 14, no. 1 (Sept. 1970).

Jones, Leroy. *Blues People: Negro Music in White America*. New York: William Morrow, 1963.

Joyce, Joyce A. "The Black Canon: Reconstructing Black American Literary Criticism." *New Literary History* 18 (1987): 335–44.

Kant, Immanuel. *Critique of Judgment*. New York: Hafner Press, 1951.

Kaplan, Gisela T., and Clive S. Kessler, eds. *Hannah Arendt*. Wellington, New Zealand: Unwin Hyman, 1989.

Kaufmann, Walter. *The Portable Nietzsche*. New York: Viking Press, 1968.

Kent, George. *Blackness and the Adventure of Western Culture*. Chicago: Third World Press, 1972.

Kesteloot, Lilyan. *Aimé Césaire*. Paris: Editions Pierre Seghers, 1962.

Kom, Ambroise. *George Lamming et le destin des Caraïbes* Montreal: Didier, 1986.

Krupnick, Mark. *Displacement: Derrida and After*. Bloomington: Indiana University Press, 1983.

Kurzweil, Edith, and William Phillips, eds. *Partisan Review* 63, no. 2 (1991).

Lacan, Jacques. *Ecrits*. New York: Norton, 1977.

———. *Feminine Sexuality*. New York: Norton, 1985.

Leiner, Jacqueline. "Entretien avec Aimé Césaire." In *Tropiques* Paris: Editions Jean-Michel Place, 1978.

Levinas, Emmanuel. *The Theory of Intuition in Husserl's Phenomenology*. Evanston: Northwestern University Press, 1973.

Lionnet, Françoise. *Autobiographical Voices*. Ithaca: Cornell University Press, 1989.

Lupton, Mary J. "Singing the Black Mother: Maya Angelou and Autobiographical Continuity." *Black American Literature Forum* 24, no. 2 (Summer 1990): 257–76.

Macksey, Richard, and Eugenio Donato, eds. *The Languages of Criticism and the Sciences of Man.* Baltimore: Johns Hopkins University Press, 1970.

Malbon, Elizabeth S. "Fallible Followers: Women and Men in the Gospel of Mark." *Semeia 28: The Bible and Feminist Hermeneutics.* Ed. Mary Ann Tolbert, 29–48. Chico, Calif.: Scholars Press, 1983.

Mbiti, John. *African Religions and Philosophy.* New York: Anchor Books, 1970.

Mezu, Okechukwu. *The Poetry of Léopold Senghor.* London: Heinemann, 1973.

McDermott, John. *The Writings of William James.* New York: Random House, 1967.

Merton, Robert K. *Social Theory and Social Structure.* Glencoe, Ill.: Free Press, 1957.

Mitchell, Juilette. *Psychoanalysis and Feminism: Freud, Reich, Laing and Women.* New York: Vintage Books, 1975.

Muller, John, and William Richardson. *Lacan and Language.* New York: International University Press,

Murray, Albert. *Stomping the Blues.* New York: McGraw-Hill, 1976.

Nietzsche, Friedrich. *On the Geneology of Morals and Ecce Homo.* New York: Vintage Books, 1969.

Nkosi, Lewis. *Home and Exile.* London: Longmans, 1965.

Ogunyemi, Chikwenye Okonjo. "Womanism: The Dynamics of the Contemporary Black Female Novel in English." *Signs* 2, no. 1 (1985): 63–80.

Olney, James, ed. *Autobiography: Essays Theoretical and Critical.* Princeton: Princeton University Press, 1980.

Owomoyela, Oyekan. "The Phantom of Nigerian Theater." *African Studies Review* 22 (1979): 43–50.

Paulson, Steve. "Scenes from the Afro-American Studies Conference." *Isthmus* 16 (May 3–9, 1991): 33–35.

Pochmann, Henry. *New England Transcendentalism and St. Louis Hegelianism: Phases in the History of American Idealism.* Philadelphia: Carl Schurz Memorial Foundation, 1948.

Pryse, Marjorie and Hortense Spillers, eds. *Conjuring: Black Women, Fiction, and Literary Tradition.* Bloomington: Indiana University Press, 1985.

Rabinow, Paul, ed. *The Foucault Reader.* New York: Pantheon Books, 1984.

Rampersad, Arnold. *The Art and Imagination of W. E. B. Du Bois.* Cambridge: Harvard University Press, 1976.

Rauch, Leo. *Hegel and the Human Spirit.* Detroit: Wayne State University Press, 1983.

Rosenblatt, Louise. "On the Aesthetic as the Basic Model of the Reading Process." *Bucknell Review* 26, no. 1 (1981): 17–32.

Schurmann, Reiner. *Heidegger on Being and Acting: From Principles to Anarchy.* Bloomington: Indiana University Press, 1987.

Senghor, Léopold. *Liberté 3: Négritude et civilisation de l'universel*. Paris: Editions du Seuil, 1977.

——. *Pour une lecture Négro-Africaine de Mallarmé*. Paris: Obsidiane, 1981.

Showalter, Elaine, ed. *Speaking of Gender*. New York: Routledge, 1989.

Simpson, Lewis, et al. *The Southern Review and Modern Literature 1935–1985*. Baton Rouge: Louisiana State University Press, 1988.

Singleton, Carrie J. "Race and Gender in Feminist Theory. *Sage* 6, no. 1 (1989): 12–17.

Soyinka, Wole. *Myth, Literature and the African World*. Cambridge: Cambridge University Press, 1976.

Spillers, Hortense. "Formalism Comes to Harlem." *Black American Literature Forum* 14, no. 2 (1982): 58–63.

Spivak, Gayatri. *In Other Worlds*. New York: Methuen, 1987.

Steady, Filomina C. *The Black Woman Cross-Culturally*. Cambridge, Mass.: Schenkman Publishing, 1981.

——. *Women in Africa and the African Diaspora*. Washington, D.C.: Howard University Press, 1987.

Stepto, Robert. *From Behind the Veil*. 2d ed. Urbana: University of Illinois Press, 1991.

Stevenson, B. *The Home Book of Quotations: Classical and Modern*. New York: Dodd, Mead, 1967.

Tate, Claudia, ed. *Black Women Writers at Work*. New York: Continuum, 1983.

Vaillant, Janet. *Black, French, and African*. Cambridge: Harvard University Press, 1990.

Vogel, Stanley. *German Literary Influences on the American Transcendentalists*. New Haven: Yale University Press, 1955.

Walker, Alice. *In Search of Our Mother's Gardens*. New York: Harcourt Brace Jovanovich, 1983.

Walker, Cheryl. "Feminist Literary Criticism and the Author." *Critical Inquiry* 16, no. 3 (1990): 551–71.

Wall, Cheryl. *Changing Our Own Words*. New Brunswick: Rutgers University Press, 1989.

Warminski, A. *Readings in Interpretation*. Minneapolis: University of Minnesota Press, 1987.

Weixlmann, Joseph, ed. *Studies in Black American Literature, Vol. III*. Greenwood, Fla.: Penkevill Publishing, 1988.

Williams, Raymond. *Marxism and Literature*. Oxford: Oxford University Press, 1977.

Williams, C. RoseGreen. "Re-writing the History of the Afro-Cuban Woman: Nancy Morejón's 'Mujer negra.'" *Afro-Hispanic Review* 8, no. 3 (1989): 7–13.

Williamson, Joel. "W. E. B. Du Bois as a Hegelian." In *What Was Freedom's Price?* Ed. David G. Sansing, 21–49. Jackson: University Press of Mississippi, 1978.

Wright, Richard. "Tradition and Industrialization." *Présence Africaine* Nos. 8–10 (Juin–Novembre 1956).
———. *White Man, Listen!* New York: Anchor Press, 1964.
———. *Native Son.* New York: Harper and Row, 1966.
———. *Black Boy.* New York: Harper and Row, 1989.

Index

Aidoo, Ama Ata, 100
African feminism, 96–98
African life-world, 35, 52, 54–55
Afrocentrism, 2, 4
Althusser, Louis, 121
Angelou, Maya, 55, 56, 57, 59–60, 70, 71, 75, 76, 80, 84, 86; and feminism, 106–7; 138, 139. See also also *I Know Why the Caged Bird Sings*
Archaeology of Knowledge, The (Foucault), 122, 124, 126, 127
Arnold, A. James, 52
Autobiography, 54, 57–60, 63
Auto-writing, 60

Bâ, Mariama, 101
Baker, Houston A., Jr., 1, 3, 9–10, 26, 50, 55, 95, 119–31, 134, 138–39, 146n28. See also *Blues, Ideology, and Afro-American Literature*
Baldwin, James, 52–54; and the Negro as Other, 56, 60. See also "Of Princes and Power"
Balibar, Etienne, 128
Barthes, Roland, 107–9, 124
Being and Time (Heidegger), 21, 36
Black Aesthetic, 2–3
Black Arts movement, 3, 8, 22, 110, 111
Black Boy (Wright), 54–55, 59, 60, 61, 64–65, 66–67, 68–70
"Black Canon, The" (Joyce), 1–5
Black feminist literary discourse, 90–92; and literary critics, 95–96, 99–100, 113–14, 116–17, 158n45
Black vernacular, 121, 128, 130, 135, 137
Black Women Writers at Work (Tate), 59
Blanchot, Maurice, 84
Bloom, Harold, 134, 135
Blues, Ideology, and Afro-American Lit-

erature (Baker), 9, 119–31, 137. *See also* Baker, Houston
Blues matrix, 119–20, 126
Braxton, Joanne, 57–58
Brooks, Gwendolyn, 29
Brown, Sterling, 51
Burke, Kenneth, 121, 127
Busia, Abena, 99–100

Carby, Hazel, 91, 95, 113–14, 115, 116
Cartesian method, 32
"Cercle non vicieux/Nonvicious Circle" (Césaire), 41–42
Césaire, Aimé, 29, 30, 31, 32, 33, 35, 41; his rejection of Négritude as an ideology, 42–43; his poetics and literary influences, 44–51, 149n33; at the Paris Congress of Black Writers and Artists, 52; and language, 82. *See also* Paris Congress of Black Writers and Artists
Chesnutt, Charles, 8
Chiasm, 126, 131, 135
Chiasmus, 134–35, 136
Christian, Barbara, 92
Circulus vitiosus, 41
Cogito ergo sum, 24
Colie, Rosalie, 118
Colonialism, 52
Condé, Maryse, 100
Conference on Afro-American Studies in the Twenty-First Century, The, 95, 113–14, 116
Conscience païdeumatique, 32, 147n5
Consciousness: in William James, 13–14; Hegel's discussion of, 15–19; Du Bois's articulation of, 26; Du Bois as a philosopher of, 28; raising, 99; woman, 102. *See also Phenomenology of Spirit*
Cooper, Anna J., 4–8, 111–12, 141n10

Paradox, 118–19
Paris Congress of Black Writers and
    Artists, The, 51–54
Persona criticism, 109
Phenomenology and ontology, 36
Phenomenology of Spirit (Hegel), 8, 14,
    15–19, 143n7
phallogocentric, 57
Plato, 26
Poetics, 5, 40, 44
*Pour une lecture Négro-Africaine de
    Mallarmé* (Senghor), 40
"Présence/Presence" (Césaire), 49–50
Pryse, Marjorie, 57
Psychoanalysis, 56, 62

Race, class, and gender, 92, 95, 104, 115
Ragland-Sullivan, Ellie, 65–66
Reflection, 35
Representation, 5, 34
Richardson, William, 71–72
Romanticism, 5, 24
Rose, Jacqueline, 61
Royce, Josiah, 12, 143n7

St. Louis Hegelians, 16, 144n15
Sandoff, Dianne, 91
Scepticism and consciousness, 18
Self-consciousness, 13, 15–19
Senghor, Léopold, 8–9; his tribute to Du
    Bois, 29–30; and German philosophy,
    31–34; his interpretation of Heidegger's
    logos, 35–36, 38–39; and Mallarmé, 40;
    his engagement with Négritude as a
    philosophy, 42; at the Paris Congress of
    Black Writers and Artists, 51–54; and
    double-consciousness, 138–39
Showalter, Elaine, 89, 92–93, 94
Signifying, 133–34
Signifying Monkey, The (Gates), 9, 119–21,
    131–37
Singleton, Carrie Jane, 158n45
Smith, Barbara, 91
Smith, Valerie, 91–91, 109–11; 139
So Long a Letter (Bâ), 101
Sorrow Songs, 26–27

Soyinka, Wole, 132
Spillers, Hortense, 63–65, 90, 91
Spirit, 13, 18, 22, 26
Spivak, Gayatri, 93–94
Sport of the Gods, The (Dunbar), 128–29
Steady, Filomena, 96–97
Stepto, Robert B., 1, 2, 11–13, 19–21, 55,
    125. See *From Behind the Veil*
Stoicism, 18
Stowe, Harriet Beecher, 5, 6–7
Structural linguistics, 56
Souls of Black Folk, The (Du Bois), 5, 11–12,
    19–28, 29, 142n1
Striving, 12, 25, 26
Surrealists, 45, 50
Symbolic order, 57, 61, 65
Symbolism, 40

Tate, Claudia, 60, 112, 116
Tell My Horse (Hurston), 111
Their Eyes Were Watching God (Hurston),
    110–11
Thomas, Bigger, 59
Toomer, Jean, 21, 51, 110
Tourgee, Albion, 6, 7
Tropiques (Césaire), 51
Turner, Darwin, 110
Turner, Victor, 129

Walker, Alice, 63, 100, 101, 102
Walker, Cheryl, 107–9
Wall, Cheryl, 90–91
Wallace, Michelle, 115
Washington, Mary Helen, 91
White, Hayden, 121, 127, 130
Willis, Susan, 91
Williamson, Joel, 13
Womanish, 88, 89
Womanism, 100–101, 102
Wright, Richard: at the 1956 Paris Con-
    gress of Black Writers and Artists,
    51–53; and the African life-world,
    54–55, 56; as autobiographer, 59–
    60; and *Black Boy,* 65, 68–69, 71; and
    double-consciousness, 138, 139
Wynter, Sylvia, 102

SANDRA ADELL is an assistant professor in
the Department of Afro-American Studies
at the University of Wisconsin-Madison.